Data-Based Decision Making 2.0

Because research and information make the difference.

Educational Research Service
1001 North Fairfax Street, Suite 500 • Alexandria, VA 22314-1587
Phone: 703-243-2100 • Toll Free: 800-791-9308
Fax: 703-243-1985 • Toll Free: 800-791-9309
Email: ers@ers.org • Web site: www.ers.org

Educational Research Service
1001 North Fairfax Street, Suite 500
Alexandria, VA 22314-1587
Phone: 703-243-2100 • Toll Free: 800-791-9308
Fax: 703-243-1985 • Toll Free: 800-791-9309
Email: ers@ers.org • Web site: www.ers.org

Educational Research Service is the nonprofit organization serving the research and information needs of the nation's preK-12 education leaders and the public. Founded by the national school management associations, ERS provides quality, objective research and information that enable education leaders to make the most effective school decisions in both day-to-day operations and long-range planning.

ERS Founding Organizations:
American Association of School Administrators
American Association of School Personnel Administrators
Association of School Business Officials International
National Association of Elementary School Principals
National Association of Secondary School Principals
National School Public Relations Association

ERS Executive Staff:
John C. Draper, Ed.D., Chief Executive Officer
Katherine A. Behrens, Chief Operating Officer

Author: Nancy Protheroe

Copyright © 2011 Educational Research Service

Portions of this book were previously published in *Data-Based Decision Making, Second Edition*, which was co-published by ERS and NAESP in 2008 as part of the *Essentials for Principals* series.

Ordering Information: Additional copies may be purchased for the base price of $26.95; ERS subscribers $19.95. Stock No. 809. ISBN: 978-0-9836011-0-4. Order from ERS, 1001 North Fairfax Street, Suite 500, Alexandria, VA 22314-1587. Phone: 800-791-9308. Fax: 800-791-9309.

Table of Contents

Chapter 1

Introduction

> "Data-driven decision making…. It reminds practitioners that their plans have a greater likelihood of succeeding if the goals and strategies within them are based on solid information and not on hunches or habit." (Center for Comprehensive School Reform and Improvement, 2006, p. 1)

The phrase "data for decision making" has been used so often in discussions of school improvement efforts that it has become almost a mantra. In general, that's a good thing. Effective use of data has been repeatedly tied to successful efforts to increase levels of student achievement. But the word effective should be stressed. It's *how* educators use data that really provides the critical link between practice and school improvement.

The "how" of data-based decision making has evolved over the past decade—thus, the title of this book, *Data-Based Decision Making 2.0*. Educators have become more sophisticated in their use of data. In part, this is due to increased availability of user-friendly data that supports principals' and teachers' use of information about student achievement. The increased emphasis on data use also brought with it more training and heightened educators' awareness of how data use can help diagnose problems and identify possible solutions. So what we're seeing today in many schools is an increase in the use of data, the types of data used, and the number of ways data are used.

Knapp, Swinnerton, Copland, and Monpas-Huber discuss this evolution in the use of data:

> An argument can be made that educational leaders have always had "data" of some kind available to them when making decisions intended to improve teaching and learning…. [However,] the data they collected was likely impressionistic and rarely systematic, complete, or sufficiently nuanced to carry the weight of important decisions. (2006, p. 2)

They go on to describe a more thoughtful and intentional approach to using data and call this "data-informed leadership" (p. 5). This phrase has important implications for principals since providing the leadership to encourage effective data use in their schools is emerging as one of principals' most important responsibilities. Love stresses the active role educators must take when using data, as "[d]ata have no meaning. Meaning is imposed through interpretation" (2009, p. xiv). Knapp et al. agree and stress that this change in terminology away from data-driven decision making signals an important shift in the way data use should be viewed. In this new framework, data are not thought to "drive" decisions. Instead, effective data use acknowledges that educators bring into the process:

...core values and insights into those aspects of the practice for which there are not yet good data, and may never be.... The notion of data-informed leadership captures the complex and often ambiguous nature of data use in educational settings. (Knapp et al., 2006, p. 6)

This notion of data also stresses that an important outcome of data analysis should be to "prompt questions and deliberations" (Knapp et al., 2006, p. 6). One school leader talks about the active role educators must take in analyzing data since "data only led you to questions, and that solutions emerge by analyzing root causes" (Datnow, Park, & Wohlstetter, 2007, p. 27):

I can give you an aspirin if you have a headache. But if your head hurts because you've had an aneurysm, then giving you aspirin isn't going to help. It's the same thing with education and data. If you don't examine the data and look deeply at the root causes, you might just be solving the wrong problem or addressing the problem the wrong way. And in the end, that won't help the students. (in Datnow et al., p. 27)

Obviously, principals will need to play a key role in developing a school culture that supports this more intensive—and often less obvious—use of data. Creighton describes it this way: "We must become more proactive and move beyond the 'on the surface' work with data—and investigate 'below the surface' issues related to our data" (2007, pp. 1-2).

> "Data can and should be used as a mechanism for having conversations about school processes, direction, results, capacity, and improvement.... Data becomes information, and information becomes knowledge when people make sense out of it through thoughtful conversations that shape the information to make it meaningful in their context. This gives them the foundation for making wise decisions based on their new knowledge." (Earl & Katz, 2008, p. 8)

Data Use and School Improvement

The term data-informed leadership stresses the active role educators must take in using data. These leaders must also work to make the link between data use and school improvement explicit. Improvement—at both the classroom and school levels—is the reason for spending time and other resources on collecting and analyzing data. Datnow et al. are clear: "The use of data is an important tool in school improvement" (2007, p. 10), with the gathering, sharing, and analysis of data core elements needed to support a "systematic approach to making continuous improvement" (2007, p. 17).

Weiss presents a cycle of school improvement (see Figure 1.1) in which data use is embedded that also stresses the ongoing nature of effective improvement efforts. She talks about this:

The term "cycle of continuous instructional improvement" describes the process by which teachers adapt instruction to meet the differing needs of their students, and by learning from experience and evidence, also improve their own

practice. Great teachers have always done this, instinc-
tively taking responsibility for the learning of each of their
students and constantly following up to see how each is
doing.... At the heart of this system is data. These data
are emphatically not the mountains of useless data every school system has today that are stuffed into binders,
pouring out of filing cabinets, and cluttering up computer
hard drives—methods that render much of it inaccessible,
unusable and out of date. The data we require are useful,
relevant, accurate, and timely, and can be trusted as the
basis for making instructional decisions. (2007, p. 5)

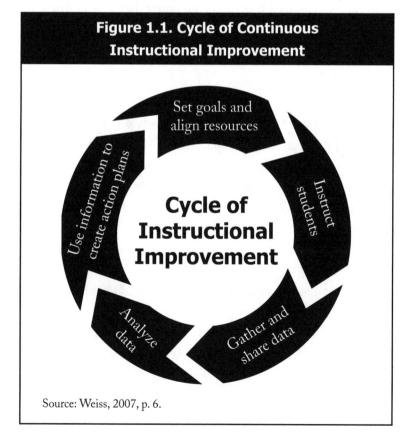

Figure 1.1. Cycle of Continuous Instructional Improvement

Set goals and align resources

Use information to create action plans

Cycle of Instructional Improvement

Instruct students

Analyze data

Gather and share data

Source: Weiss, 2007, p. 6.

Killion and Bellamy also stress the importance of data to school improvement. They suggest that "because data abound, schools must become data savvy":

> Without analyzing and discussing data, schools are unlikely to identify and solve the problems that need attention, identify appropriate interventions to solve those problems, or know how they are progressing toward achievement of their goals. Data are the fuel of reform.... In short, using data separates good schools from mediocre schools. Schools that are increasing student achievement, staff productivity and collegiality, and customer satisfaction use data to inform and guide their decisions and actions. Data use essentially sets a course of action and keeps a staff on that course to school improvement and student success. (2000)

Aldersebaes, Potter, and Hamilton speak of "using data to ignite change" (2000, p. 20), with school staff using "meaningful" data to:

- uncover needs, priorities, and resources;
- build a school profile to better understand the school's strengths and weaknesses;
- develop intrinsic motivation through identifying a need for change;
- create a focused direction for change accompanied by realistic goals; and,
- establish a baseline against which to measure progress and design a plan to evaluate programs or practices.

The bottom line—it makes sense to use data to help clarify decisions, identify alternative solutions to problems, and target resources more effectively. The real question should not be *whether* to integrate the use of data in school improvement, but *how*. However, identifying good data and using it effectively is a complex process, one that some schools are just beginning to address.

Data-Based Decision Making 2.0 is designed to help principals take on the role of data-informed leadership. The how-to's of building a school culture in which data use is seen as a natural and necessary part of a process of continuous improvement will be discussed. One aspect of this development will be addressing important preconditions such as staff education in data use. Another is putting in place some of the nuts and bolts of effective data use.

The discussion will then turn to several ways principals, teachers, and other staff members can develop and use data to support improvement of instruction and other school functions. Each of these chapters is organized around three commonsense, practical questions:

- What are we looking for?
- How will we look for it?
- How will we use the data?

Embedded throughout this book will be references to the important role principals play in moving their schools toward effective data use. You will need to provide support for the process as well as demonstrate your commitment to use of data in decision making. We hope the content provided here will help you do these things effectively.

An experienced teacher working in a school with an ethnically and economically diverse student population talks about the impact of effective data use on student learning:

[Our new principal] believed that everything (the current status, the efforts undertaken to improve it, and all progress made) must be measurable. He led the staff, students, and community into sharing his goals . . . and can verify, via measurable data, that the students are doing much, much better. I firmly believe that managing data was key to [our school's] academic rebirth, so to speak. All of us teaching there cared deeply for the students and wanted them to learn, but researching and managing data is what got us unified in our approach and able to verify the successes of our efforts. (Pam_I_Am, 2007)

Implications for Our School: Questions for Discussion and Reflection

- How would we describe our school's current approach to using data?
- Do we use data to help drive continuous improvement in classrooms and schoolwide?
- Do we make use of a variety of data sources, or do we rely too heavily on information from standardized assessments?

Follow-up and Action Items

_____

_____

_____

_____

_____

_____

_____

_____

_____

_____

_____

_____

_____

_____

_____

_____

_____

_____

Chapter 2

Preconditions for Effective Data Use

"One thing is crystal clear from the research to date: where it occurs, data-informed leadership is a direct reflection of aggressive, persistent attempts by leaders to create conditions in which this way of approaching the business of schooling can flourish." (Knapp et al., 2006, p. 37)

Studies of data use in schools make it clear that some schools do it more effectively. The context in which data is used is a variable that can have a substantial effect on this. Thornton and Perreault talk about "necessary prior conditions" for successful data-based leadership. In their view,

> These conditions include a shared vision, a trust-filled environment, and a principal who understands data. If these are not present within the school, then it is essential that they be developed before proceeding, because their absence will significantly undermine any data-based efforts to improve the school. (2002, p. 87)

Principal leadership is embedded in ensuring "prior conditions" are present. However, there are other ways in which a principal can develop an environment supportive of data use. Thornton and Perreault talk about this:

> Demonstrating the utility of data is critical to gaining teachers' support and cooperation. In general, teachers need to become comfortable consumers; the data collected should become 'their' data.... By engaging staff members in a meaningful project, the principal can identify and model the value of data-based decision making....To build teachers' confidence in data analysis, the principal should select an initial project that is likely to succeed. (2002, p. 90)

Holcomb (2004) identifies some barriers to data use she has observed in her work with educators. These barriers include:

- lack of training—including time to practice with use of the data as well as skill acquisition
- lack of time—specifically time to work collaboratively
- feast or famine—the sense in the beginning that needed data are not available, often followed by the feeling of being swamped with data
- fear of evaluation
- fear of exposure since work with data often moves people out of their comfort zones
- confusing a technical problem with a cultural problem—specifically, effective data analysis requires "accepting collective responsibility for the learning of students" (p. 32) in addition to number crunching.

Explicitly addressing these barriers can help to provide more fertile ground for the growth of data-informed decision making. Johnson (2002) suggests that a school staff include self-reflection in its planning. For example, "What do you perceive as your major issues and roadblocks around engaging in data use?" "What strengths do you bring to the table around data use?" "What kinds of professional development do you need to become a more effective user of data?"

Now, let's move ahead to discussing some of the essential preconditions for effective schoolwide data use.

A Trusting Environment

It's easy to see why some staff members might fear increased use of data since it can shine a brighter light on school problems or on personal lack of success with helping particular students achieve. Thus, your role as principal in developing a trusting environment needs to begin long before you increase your emphasis on data use.

As an example of the importance of trust to data use, Langer, Colton, and Goff talk about teachers engaged in collaborative analysis of student work: "Trust in fellow group members allows you to bring a struggling student's work to the group without fear of being judged or criticized" (2003, p. 46).

Training for Staff

Obviously, teachers and other staff members will need support—especially training—in how to address these important functions. This element has been addressed head-on by schools that have incorporated the effective use of data in their improvement efforts. Opportunities to learn how to analyze assessment data have typically been provided in a variety of ways, including:

- staff development focused on how to "read" and analyze reports of assessment results;
- presentations by central office staff or principals to school staff, followed by a discussion of possible next steps;
- one-on-one sessions of a principal, assistant principal, or lead teacher with a teacher to review and discuss results from classes and students; and,
- training of an in-school data expert, typically a teacher, who works with grade-level or subject-area teams to analyze the data.

However, Holcomb reminds us that effective data use requires more than number-crunching skills. For this reason,

The ability, capacity, and commitment to use data cannot be developed through training in the traditional sense of courses and workshops. It is far more complex than individual knowledge and skill acquisition, and it must be embedded in the ongoing work of groups of professionals. (2004, p. 30)

Thus, training is often especially powerful when it is organized around an authentic task. When teachers are carefully supported through their initial efforts to use assessment data to improve classroom instruction, they are simultaneously learning important skills. Reeves (2004) talks about a process that could fill this dual purpose role of data use and training:

- Have faculty agree on the "12 most important standards for each subject, each grade." One way to accelerate the process is to have teachers answer this question: "What knowledge and skills do students need in the next lower grade in order to come into your class with confidence and success next year?" Whereas 5th grade teachers may not be able to narrow the focus for themselves, they have little trouble in narrowing the focus for 4th grade.

- Have faculty teams design very short assessments that, over the course of a year, address these brief sets of power standards. "Very short" means about 15 items, 12 multiple choice, and 3 extended response. This should not take more than 20 minutes of classroom time each month, and the grading can be immediate.

- Provide some time in faculty meetings or already scheduled group time to grade the three quick extended response items. Ensure that the credit given is consistent—that is, faculty members can look at an anonymous piece of student work and agree on whether or not it is "proficient" and what credit it should receive.

- Provide time in faculty meetings after each assessment has been graded to get very clear answers to this question: "Based on the results we have just observed, how will the next few weeks and months be different in terms of schedule, curriculum, and teaching strategies?"

Finally, training for staff should include time spent on encouraging teachers and other school staff to recognize the data analysis skills they already have. Earl and Katz talk directly to educators who feel they "cannot do this 'data stuff'" because they are no good with math." They stress that "data literacy is not the same as 'crunching numbers'" (2006, p. 45) and go on to describe what they mean by data literacy. It is a thinking process—a process of:

- standing back and deciding what you need to know and why;
- collecting or locating the necessary data;
- finding ways to link key data sources, ensuring that the data are worth considering;
- being aware of their limitations;
- thinking about what the results mean; and, finally,
- systematically considering an issue from a range of perspectives so that you really feel that you have evidence to explain, support, and also challenge your point of view. (Earl & Katz, 2006, p. 45)

For principals, learning how to analyze and use the data often requires aligning this knowledge with other supervisory skills. For example, a principal interviewed by Cromey and Hanson (2000) reported using assessment data to:

identify, then intervene with teachers whose students consistently performed lower on a variety of assessments compared to other teachers. The principal indicated that these data neutralize potentially daunting conversations by providing objective information that can be further probed to identify more specific instructional needs. Further, attempts by the teacher to improve his or her teaching can be evaluated with the same data. The principal acknowledged that many teachers have had negative experiences when using student data because they have been "hit over the head with it." Therefore, the principal used data constructively and attempted to frame these conversations proactively.

> "Colleagues sitting down to look at and discuss student work . . . are practicing an essential form of assessment data collection." (Gregory & Kuzmich, 2004, p. 69)

Opportunities for Teachers to Collaborate

Another key component of effective systems of data use is the provision of time for teachers to discuss the data and to work together to develop solutions. For teachers, this time provides an opportunity both to develop their skills in data analysis and to brainstorm and share effective instructional strategies. While common planning time is often difficult to provide, Cromey and Hanson describe systems used in four schools they visited (see Table 2.1).

Table 2.1.   Scheduling Approaches for Teacher Collaboration

	School A	School B	School C	School D
Time and Planning Strategies	Once every month, the school day begins two hours later—teachers meet during this time to engage in the activities described below. School makes up this accumulated time by extending the school year.	School staff are released early from school once per week for at least 45 minutes. This time is added to other days throughout the week. Entire staff meets once a week for one hour before school. Staff decreased the "nuts and bolts" of the meetings and prioritized work related to assessment.	Same-grade teachers meet informally during weekly planning periods and formally every six weeks. To accommodate these planning periods, students in entire grades are sent to "specials" (e.g., gym, art classes). Time is also allotted at regularly scheduled staff meetings. Teachers are released from teaching duties several days each year and are replaced by substitute teachers. Teachers meet with the principal up to three times each year.	Teachers request time to meet with each other during school hours; substitutes are hired to support this. In addition, teachers meet after school. Teachers meet in "within-grade" and "subject-area" teams during their planning hours once per week.
Activities	School staff rewrite district standards and realign the assessments they use accordingly. School staff continuously re-evaluate this work, and discuss and plan changes as needed.	Schools use allotted time to align curriculum across grades and with the state standards. This process is driven by student assessment data. School staff continuously re-evaluate this work and discuss and plan changes as needed.	Staff discuss students' progress according to the "developmental continuums" written by school staff. Teachers administer individual assessments to students. Staff discuss reports on assessment data from district research department.	Staff share knowledge gained from professional development activities that addressed curriculum and assessment. They also discuss student mastery of standards and other outcomes and possible intervention strategies.

Source: Cromey & Hanson, 2000

"For practitioners to develop a commitment to data use . . . school cultures that trust data and support high-quality data use must be nurtured." (Heritage & Yeagley, 2005, p. 334)

Developing a Culture of Data Use

Principals who want to build a culture of data use in their schools must look first to themselves. Ask yourself, am I demonstrating use of data in making decisions—or do staff members only hear me talking about the importance of using it? You should be modeling use of data every day.

One challenge to principals working to build a schoolwide program of data use may be breaking down the closed-door culture of teaching. Boudett and Moody talk about the importance of making data study a collaborative approach from the very beginning:

> Even in cases where one person is willing to assume primary responsibility for data work, it is important that that person not work alone. Assembling a group of people, assigning responsibility for specific tasks, and planning how individuals will coordinate their efforts with each other and the rest of the school sends a message that using data in your school will be a collaborative effort. (Boudett & Moody, 2005, p. 14)

Finally, the relationship of school culture and data use often is a two-way process. As teachers learn to use data, it not only becomes second nature—it begins to affect other aspects of their teaching in a positive way:

> In learning to incorporate data analysis as a regular part of their professional activity, teachers become more reflective about their teaching practices, less reactive, less willing to accept easy answers, and more open-minded to solutions based on the data they gather. (Wade, 2001, p. 2)

Implications for Our School:
Questions for Discussion and Reflection

- Do we have roadblocks that limit our effective use of data?
- What are our strengths related to data use?
- Do we need additional professional development to become more effective in our use of data? If so, what should it look like?

Follow-up and Action Items

_____

_____

_____

_____

_____

_____

_____

_____

_____

_____

_____

_____

_____

_____

_____

_____

_____

_____

_____

Chapter 3

Developing a Process

> "At its best, data should be more than a number. It should tell stories. Measure capacity. Create, in a sense, a living picture in order to see the school and the system in a different way. Present 'the everyday' in a precise and meaningful way." (School leader from a district participating in a project of the Annenberg Institute for School Reform in Mishook, Foley, Thompson, & Kubiak, 2008)

A major shift in how schools use data—part of the evolution to data-based decision making 2.0—involves how tightly effective data-using schools have embedded data use in their everyday work. This is important since:

> for data analysis to ultimately have an impact on student achievement, it needs to be part of a cyclical process. When data analysis is viewed as one step in a system, its use will become integral to the workings of an organization. Without a process, data analysis can be only an event. Time is spent viewing and analyzing data, but there is no intended result other than to comment on what is observed. Although time is not wasted, data viewed without a process will not likely become a catalyst for change. (Depka, 2006, p. 2)

Some schools are already sophisticated data users. They have developed approaches that work for them—yielding good information and making effective use of staff time. However, other schools want to increase data use and want to move forward without stumbling. Gregory and Kuzmich (2004) suggest that more successful approaches often start small, and City, Kagle, and Teoh suggest that principals working to establish a more comprehensive approach to data use in their schools first ask themselves:

> How much time do you have to collect and analyze the data? What other resources do you have available to you? The answers to these questions influence how many data sources you can examine and which ones you choose. (2005, p. 113)

Schmoker agrees and provides some concrete suggestions for a school that wants to become more effective in its use of data to improve instruction:

> Concentrate on three very simple things—focused, collaborative learning, measurable goals, and data. Begin by looking at the data to establish one or two measurable goals. Have teachers get together in the summer when they have time and can be more relaxed to select or create periodic assessments by which they will measure progress related to that goal. Then have teams of teachers get together regularly to talk about their progress, focusing like a laser beam on specific emergent problems preventing students from doing well relative to that year-end goal. If a school does these things, it is all but certain to make some real progress. (in Sparks, 2000)

Johnson suggests that "a logical first step in using data is to begin making better use of existing data. A systematic analysis of data that are already being collected can reveal previously unseen patterns and opportunities for improvement" (2000). Depka has another suggestion in regard to data use and advises principals to guard against a "the more, the merrier" approach to data use:

> Be selective about the data you choose . . . The data you select should relate to your goal. If the plan is to analyze student academic achievement, choose the sources that will give you the best all-around indications. It is important to provide enough data so that participants can have a good degree of confidence that their observations are accurate. Too much information at one data delve can overwhelm, confuse, and exhaust people. There is certainly a time and place to view it all, but the data should be viewed in segments to avoid data overload. (2006, p. 22)

"Before you can move effectively toward your desired future, you need a firm understanding of where you are. Gathering data helps you understand and describe your current reality." (Cervone & Martinez-Miller, 2007, p. 2)

Keeping the very real constraints of time—especially teacher time—in mind is obviously important. Thus, while some approaches to data collection and analysis may, by their nature, require fairly intensive investments of time, other approaches can be easy to implement while providing helpful data. For example, Depka suggests that teachers use color-coding when recording low scores in a grade book. The use of different colors "creates a visual of those in need of occasional support and identifies students who are experiencing repeated difficulties" (2006, p. 69). This visual could be helpful to teachers when planning instruction and can also provide data for teacher-principal meetings on student progress or a discussion among teachers working to identify strategies to use with students having difficulty.

Finally, City et al. discuss trade-offs principals may need to consider as they begin schoolwide data use initiatives:

> If you examine instruction more quickly with limited data sources, you will get to designing and implementing solutions faster, but you may sacrifice some accuracy in understanding the teaching dimensions of the problem of practice. If you take your time and examine several data sources, you may be more accurate, but you may lose a sense of urgency and momentum for improvement.... If you have a few people do most of the examining instruction work, you may get it done more quickly and at greater depth, but you may not get the level of understanding and buy-in you'll want from the rest of the teachers whose practice you ultimately want to improve. (2005, p. 114)

"Researchers studying schools and other workplaces have found that leaders who are most successful at transforming their organizations are those who know how to frame important questions and then engage their colleagues in finding creative answers." (Boudett & Steele, 2007, p. 2)

Love talks about the use of data for school improvement as both a challenge and an opportunity (2009, p. ix) and stresses that effective data use—not just going through the motions—is needed to support school improvement since, "Simply having more data available is not sufficient. Schools are drowning in data. The problem is marshaling data as the powerful force for change they are" (Love, 2009, p. ix).

> "Data alone do not answer questions; instead, they provide decision makers with additional information to think with as they consider complex educational issues from a range of vantage points." (Earl & Katz, 2010, p. 10)

Ultimately, your goal should be to integrate the use of data in the day-to-day operations of your school and as part of a continuous cycle of school improvement. Thornton and Perreault describe the alignment of data use with a cycle of school improvement. Note how data collection and use are embedded in their description of the cycle:

- **Develop a plan.** The plan should focus data collection efforts on a specific systemic issue or issues. What data will be collected? How will we improve the system? What new instructional methods or procedure will be developed? What is the current baseline on critical measures? What staff development is needed?

- **Implement the plan.** Did we successfully implement the plan? How well is the plan working? Do staff members need further professional development? Regular assessments should be conducted. At this stage, it is crucial to monitor implementation, collect data, and provide feedback.

- **Analyze the results.** Are staff members working collaboratively? Are staff members exhibiting skills and confidence in data analysis….When determining whether the implementation is successful, criteria to consider are disaggregation of data, performance-based summaries, and open discussions.

- **Take action.** What have we learned? How can we improve the system? What adjustments in the system do the data suggest? (Excerpted from Thornton & Perreault, 2002, pp. 92-93)

Implications for Our School:
Questions for Discussion and Reflection

- Could our process of data use be described as well organized? Or is it often hit and miss?
- Do we use staff time effectively?
- What are some specific ways we can improve?

Follow-up and Action Items

_____

_____

_____

_____

_____

_____

_____

_____

_____

_____

_____

_____

_____

_____

_____

_____

_____

_____

Chapter 4

Using Data to Assess the Effectiveness of School Programs

"Evaluation, at its core, is simple and useful: Finding what works and what doesn't." (Kaufman, Guerra, & Platt, 2006, p. 1)

One important use of data in schools is in evaluation of programs. The word program here is used broadly. It could apply to something as large as an after-school tutoring program, perhaps a particular approach to teaching reading, or maybe something narrower such as the use of a specific instructional strategy. The important point is that schools—and, especially, you as the school's leader—should be constantly looking at what staff members are doing and then asking: "Is it having a positive impact on students?"

Program evaluation can help to answer a range of common-sense—but critically important—questions. For example, "Are things going as planned?" "Are we beginning to see the results we anticipated?" "What changes should we make, if any, to ensure success?" (Mid-continent Research for Education and Learning, 2000). Cicchinelli and Barley (1999) suggest that evaluations can also focus on another essential element of program effectiveness and ask the question, "Did you do what you intended to?" This is a particularly important question in schools since a program or approach that has previously been effective in other settings can be ineffective in yours if the way it is being implemented takes it far away from the program's intended design. Guskey adds some additional perspectives on questions an evaluation can address:

> We use evaluations to determine the value of something—to help answer such questions as, Is this program or activity achieving its intended results? Is it better than what was done in the past? Is it better than another, competing activity? Is it worth the costs? (2002, p. 46)

Finally, Howard steps back from the idea of evaluating one specific program and puts the approach in a broader context:

> School improvement and data-driven decision making are two terms that all school leaders hear almost every day. Program evaluation brings together these two concepts by focusing data collection and analysis in an organized way in order to improve programs and, through improvement of these component programs, to improve schools. (2004, p. 1)

"Quite simply, evaluation means taking a closer look at and getting feedback about an undertaking, with an eye to making a decision about its value. In schools, program evaluation means examining initiatives the school has undertaken—whether the initiative is an approach to literacy instruction or a program to support struggling students—to answer the question, 'Is what we are doing working?'" (Center for Comprehensive School Reform and Improvement, 2006, p. 2)

Just What IS This Thing Called Evaluation, Anyway?

Consider this interchange:

"How did you like that restaurant we went to?"

"I thought it was good. The fish was very fresh, caught today. The servings were huge! And the menu was great—over 20 selections. How about you? What did you think?"

"Well, it didn't impress me much. The waiter took over 10 minutes just to bring us water. And they were all out of the blueberry pie!"

"Hmm, I gave it high marks and you flunked it. I guess we need to go back again to get some more data!"

We have just witnessed an evaluation taking place. It happens all the time. Which fruit to buy? Which shirt to wear? What TV program to watch? You are an evaluator. We are all evaluators. Evaluation is so much a part of everyday life that we often don't even notice when we are doing it. It is a necessary part of our lives and a skill that we need to survive, as well as to better our lives. If the fish in the restaurant had not been cooked properly and we incorrectly evaluated it as fresh, that would definitely be a threat to our health.

Evaluation is simply judging the value of something.

Program evaluation is simply making this same kind of judgment about a program. Is it being carried out correctly (did the water arrive on time)? Is it having the kinds of effects it set out to accomplish (were the servings adequate)? What were the activities (the menu)? What were the outcomes (how did the meal taste)?

How do we make these kinds of judgments? We gather evidence. Some things are easier to gather evidence about than others. How long the waiter took to bring us water can be measured with a wristwatch. And either they had blueberry pie or they did not. Yes or no. When it is something like this, that can be measured by anyone and the answer would be the same, we call it "objective" evidence. Some things are more difficult to measure. How fresh was the fish? How do we know? By the color? By the texture? Maybe by the waiter telling us it was caught today! When the available evidence is that of our senses we call it "subjective."

When we are evaluating educational programs, usually the more objective the evidence, the better. Evaluating a textbook or a new teaching technique, for example, can involve some pretty heavy consequences. We don't want our kids "eating a poisonous fish"; we want their educational meal to be adequate and nutritious! (Excerpted from Hammond, 2006, p. 11)

But We Can't Do a Program Evaluation!

While you might agree in theory with the idea that data should be collected to assess how well programs are working, you might also be thinking, "We don't have the time or skills needed for this evaluation 'thing'?" You are definitely not alone in that opinion.

> Many believe that evaluation is a highly unique and complex process that occurs at a certain time in a certain way, and almost always includes the use of outside experts. Many people believe they must completely understand terms such as validity and reliability. They don't have to. They do have to consider what information they need in order to make current decisions about program issues or needs. And they have to be willing to commit to understanding what is really going on.... [Otherwise,] they miss precious opportunities to make more of a difference for their customer and clients, or to get a bigger bang for their buck. (McNamara, 1998)

Herman and Winters suggest that educators' long-term experience as "progress trackers" who gather a range of data intended to help assess what is going on in classrooms prepares them well for program evaluation. They continue, "Much of this progress tracking, whether at the classroom or program level, addresses two simple questions: How are we doing? How can we improve?" (1992, p. 7).

McNamara agrees that educators have the skills and ability to conduct evaluations, since they:

do not have to be experts in these topics to carry out a useful program evaluation. The '20-80' rule applies here, that 20% of effort generates 80% of the needed results. It's better to do what might turn out to be an average effort at evaluation than to do no evaluation at all. (McNamara, 1998)

In addition, "many evaluation techniques are easy to execute; can make use of data that are already being gathered; and can be performed on a scale that is practical for teachers, principals, and other school leaders" (Center for Comprehensive School Reform and Improvement, 2006, pp. 1-2).

> "Good evaluations don't have to be complicated. They simply require thoughtful planning, the ability to ask good questions, and a basic understanding of how to find valid answers." (Guskey, 2002, p. 46)

Most schools don't have the resources to hire an outside person to help with a program evaluation—but are also concerned about the staff time it will take. Howard addresses the resource issue. In her view, an evaluation can be organized to make efficient use of staff time. In addition, developing the skills for program evaluation among school staff produces an additional benefit: it helps to build a school culture of reflective practice and continuous improvement.

The challenge, then, is to conduct an evaluation so it yields useful data—while not diverting undue amounts of staff time from teaching and other important responsibilities. We again will use our three questions—What Are We Looking For? How Will We Look For It? How Will We Use the Data?—to help structure the process.

"It helps to be clear about what a program is and is not. A program is a planned, developed, or adopted set of procedures intended to deliver mastery of concepts, knowledge, skills, attitudes, or behaviors for students. To know whether a program is useful, it must be evaluated to see if it does what it is intended to do effectively and whether it is worth its cost, time, effort, and support." (Downey, Steffy, Poston, & English, 2009, p. 96)

What Are We Looking For?

Obviously, you will have some very specific questions you are attempting to answer. However, it might be helpful to look first at some broad purposes of program evaluation and use these to help define your questions—in essence, the purpose of your evaluation. Howard talks about these purposes, nothing that a program evaluation can focus on any or all of the following:

- **Assessing program efficacy.** Is the program or activity demonstrating effectiveness? Is the program meeting its stated goals and objectives? Of course, it is most useful to focus on such questions when the program has clearly defined goals and objectives.

- **Taking stock.** How well is the program being implemented? Are there variations across classrooms? Do particular components seem to be strengthening the overall program? How has the addition of technology affected the reading program's effectiveness? Have students using a newly introduced software program, intended to strengthen phonemic awareness, demonstrated higher achievement in reading? Has student motivation increased with the use of a particular software program?

- **Problem solving.** If the program seems to have problems, what is the nature of the problems and what are some possible solutions? For example, if you already know from discussions with teachers that some teachers are highly satisfied with the reading program, while others have less positive opinions, a well-designed program evaluation might help to identify the source of these differing opinions. Perhaps the more positive teachers received better training in use of the program. Or perhaps the program is more successful with some students than with others, and the dissatisfied teachers are concerned about the students who are falling behind. (Howard, 2004, p. 6)

Howard also talks about the importance of carefully defining the purpose of the evaluation:

An ill-defined purpose can result in ambiguous or off-target findings that do not enhance decision making. A question that is too narrowly defined may lead to results that are meaningless at a programmatic level. Conversely, a question that is too broadly defined may lead to contradictory or even incoherent results. (Howard, 2004, p. 18)

Program Evaluation for Decision Making:
Links in a Chain

A critical component of planning is defining the purpose of the evaluation. A clear purpose will make it easier to develop and clarify the research questions so that you can gather appropriate evidence to support the eventual decision making that will follow the evaluation. You may find it helpful to think of each of these steps as a link in a chain. As each link is strengthened, the chain itself becomes stronger. The stronger the chain, the more useful the overall evaluation becomes as a tool for program improvement.

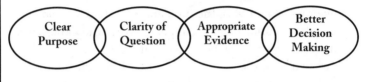

Source: Howard 2004, p. 17-18

Formative Evaluations

Although many formal program evaluations may be summative in nature—for example, asking whether a program met its goals—formative evaluations are likely to be most helpful to your school's improvement efforts. There is a commonsense reason for this. Periodic reviews of how things are going can help you ensure that programs, use of specific teaching strategies, etc., are headed in the right direction. Formative evaluations can help:

- determine whether the program is being implemented as the program developers designed it and that the most vital components of the program are in place

- enable staff to retool and fine-tune their efforts to make a program work at a specific site. A strong formative evaluation can help a program to "hum" at a particular school. (Yap, Aldersebaes, Railsback, Shaughnessy, & Speth, 2000, p. 19)

Both of these elements are particularly important to a school staff's efforts to implement a program new to the school or a particular group of teachers.

Developing Key Questions

Certainly, you will have a purpose for the evaluation—one that may be broad or fairly narrowly focused. But it is the question creation step that really defines the evaluation. The importance of spending time and careful thought developing these cannot be overstated, since "ultimately, the way the questions are worded will affect the kinds of conclusions that can be drawn about the program" (Yap et al., 2000, p. 24). They will also affect the kinds of data that will be needed and how data will need to be analyzed. Questions should be clear, specific, pertinent to essential aspects or components of implementation of the program, and focused on a manageable set of issues (Yap et al., 2000).

How Will We Look For It?

The "how" should begin with developing a thorough plan of action. Just as we know that teachers are more effective when they develop comprehensive lesson plans, an evaluation will be more effective and easier to conduct when you spend time on careful and detailed planning. As part of the planning process, you will need to:

- Establish due dates and timelines. Be realistic when assigning the amount of time needed—both staff hours and calendar time—for specific aspects of the evaluation. Planning too tightly almost guarantees that there will be slippage, and the overall project may suffer.

- Identify resources to aid in the evaluation. Although you may already have had some discussions about the resources available for the project, it is important at this stage to begin to align those resources with elements of the evaluation. Staff time and expertise are two resources that should be discussed in detail at this stage.

- Identify the components of the evaluation and assign responsibilities. Obviously the components of every program evaluation will be unique. The important thing at this stage is to think concretely—and in as detailed a manner as possible—about what will need to be done. As principal, you have had experience with managing complex tasks. The evaluation team will need your expertise during this phase. If the team talks only in generalities about what will need to be done and fails to focus on the details, stop the discussion and use some examples to demonstrate the level of planning needed.

One important piece of advice: Keep the plan as simple as possible, especially for your first program evaluation. Remember that everyone working on the evaluation has other responsibilities, and that the evaluation will need to mesh with the normal flow of school work.

Data Needed for the Evaluation

Once the key questions have been identified, the staff members working on the evaluation can focus on deciding what information (data) will be needed to answer them. In Champion's view,

There are no Swiss army knives when it comes to data. No single data source can measure everything.... A good evaluation includes several kinds of data that measure the same thing from different angles. (2002)

But, trying to draw from too many data sources may prove confusing. The goal is to develop an evaluation plan that balances the need for information with ease and cost of data collection. To do this, you must decide what information is critical to answering the question. You may also find that some of the relevant data may be difficult or expensive (in terms of time and money) to collect. Circle back to your questions and ask whether different ones—ones that could be addressed more economically—would still provide you with a productive evaluation.

> "One of the fundamental principles of program evaluation is that the evaluation should not be done if it is not going to be used." (Sanders & Sullins, 2006, p. 59)

When considering evidence for an evaluation, most people think of information that can be counted or measured numerically— student grades, standardized test scores, attendance records, and so on. It can be very useful because it is often easy to obtain and can be analyzed using statistical techniques. However, descriptions of how the program functions or the feelings and attitudes of those involved with the program also may be useful data to collect. Data of this sort can provide context and help to explain what the program means to those involved with it. Qualitative information may include surveys, interviews, or observations.

One school scheduled weekly staff development breakout sessions focused on introducing teachers to new instructional strategies or discussing ones they were already using. Short evaluations were used as a way to keep the quality of these programs high and the content relevant to teachers' needs.

Wednesday Morning Breakout Session Evaluation

Date: _____

Session: _____

The topic was timely and applicable.	❑ Yes	❑ No
The information presented was useful.	❑ Yes	❑ No
I would like another session on this topic.	❑ Yes	❑ No
I would recommend this session to a colleague.	❑ Yes	❑ No

The best part of the session was:

_____
_____
_____

Something I would change about the session is:

_____
_____
_____

(Standerfer, 2005, p.18)

How Will We Use the Data?

Using the data is a must-do step of any evaluation. Otherwise, the resources used to support it would have been better "spent" elsewhere. This step of using the data has two components—analyzing it in order to glean "lessons" from it and then using these lessons to support decision making about next steps. Killion talks about the first component:

> Interpretation is the "meaning-making" process that comes after the data have been counted, sorted, analyzed, and displayed. (2002, p. 109)

McNamara suggests that this meaning-making should begin with the goals of your evaluation—the questions you wanted to answer:

> This will help you organize your data and focus your analysis. For example, if you wanted to improve your program by identifying its strengths and weaknesses, you can organize data into program strengths, weaknesses, and suggestions to improve the program. (1998)

Using the Results of Your Analysis: The Critical Questions

- Are participant outcome objectives being attained?
- If not, why not?
- What factors contributed to attainment of objectives?
- What factors were barriers to attainment of objectives? (Administration for Children and Families, 2003)

Here are some additional "tips" that can help you and the other staff members when analyzing the data that has been collected:

- Ask: "Do these results make sense? How can they help in decision making about the program?"
- Look at your data from a variety of perspectives. Talking about the information in team meetings may result in a broader and deeper understanding of its meaning than solitary analysis.
- Don't rush this step of the evaluation process. The first "fact" discovered may not be the most important one.
- Don't assume the program is the only source of outcomes (both positive and negative).
- Don't make too much of small differences between groups. A factor such as nonresponse bias may be contributing to this difference.
- Don't overgeneralize the findings. They should reflect only the data gathered and analyzed in the evaluation. (Cicchinelli & Barley, 1999; W.K. Kellogg Foundation, 1998)

Applying Data to Decision Making

One of the uses of program evaluation data is to inform decision making about school programs. In schools that engage in a cycle of continuous improvement, the analysis of evidence—not opinions or unsupported beliefs—drives decision making (Jandris, 2001). Depending on the purpose of the evaluation, the team will need to consider the following.

- Does the program do what it is supposed to do?

- What program improvements do the findings suggest? If you decide to keep the current program, perhaps with modifications, the findings may suggest some program improvements.

- If the evaluation provides solid data that a program isn't working—and likely will not work, what does the evaluation tell you about what to look for in a new program?

An Arlington, Virginia, Public Schools' overview of its evaluation process includes some key points that should be part of the discussion of data analysis and the reporting of data. The key points include: the ways in which the programs or services should be improved, revised, continued, or discontinued by addressing the relative effectiveness of the approach; the worth or merit of that which was evaluated; recommendations regarding continuity and revisions; and recommendations for next steps (Arlington Public Schools, 1999, pp. 3-4).

Common Challenges to Evaluation

- Lack of time and resources
- Lack of training in "practical" program evaluation
- Fear of evaluation

Source: Yap et al., 2000

What Not To Do

The process we have been discussing requires careful planning, attention to detail, and your leadership to ensure it is done well. We have focused on the to-do's of good practice. However, looking at factors that can result in an ineffective evaluation can also help in your planning efforts. McNeely (2006) lists what she describes as "common evaluation mistakes." The evaluation:

- is conducted primarily as a "final product" with no follow-up action;
- doesn't fit the specific school improvement goals of the projects;
- doesn't assign strong focus to student achievement outcomes;
- doesn't give strong focus to schools' (i.e., teachers') ability to implement the program;
- report is not written in a format to inform practice; or,
- forgets that its purpose is to be a critical friend.

Finally, Kaufman et al. stress that "evaluation data must be used for improving and never blaming" (2006, p. 2).

Other Ways You Can Help Support the Process

One way principals can help the process of program evaluation go smoothly is to build their own and staff knowledge about it (Howard, 2004). Howard provides some possible resources:

- **Literature on evaluation**. Books, articles, Web sites, and "how to" handbooks may include tips that can make some of your tasks easier.

- **School staff**. Often, you can find previously unidentified expertise in a school that might be helpful to conducting an evaluation.

- **Communication with peers**. You may want to ask other principals/administrators how they conducted a program evaluation. What did they learn? Were there any pitfalls? How did they manage the time commitment?

- **Universities/colleges of education**. If you are located near a college of education, it might be helpful to ask whether a faculty member might be interested in helping, or whether your program evaluation could be used as a student project. (Howard, 2004, p. 33)

In Howard's opinion, principals can also be pivotal in creating "evaluation-friendly" environments in their schools and offers some guidelines:

- Work to help staff understand that the intent is to evaluate programs, not people.

- Ask program planners how they plan to evaluate the success of the program and to routinely build plans for evaluation into every program.

- Integrate data collection into existing procedures as much as possible. This will limit evaluation-related disruptions.

- Coordinate data collection procedures so that multiple evaluation questions can be answered.

- Make it clear that not all program evaluations need to be broad-based. Some important questions can be addressed quite easily. (2004, p. 68)

Howard also suggests that you take some time after the evaluation to evaluate *it*. For example,

> If the results of the evaluation did not provide helpful information, then take some time to analyze how this happened. Perhaps critical data was unexpectedly unavailable—or perhaps there were flaws in the design of the evaluation. If the latter is true, it is especially important to identify problems and ways to ensure these will not happen again during another evaluation. (2004, p. 67)

Champion stresses that it is important that your initial efforts to conduct more systematic reviews of your school's programs be of high quality—even if that means they are fairly limited in scope:

> Think big, but take some small, carefully considered steps. Start with a conversation with your colleagues about what would be most useful to know with some certainty.... You don't need to do everything at once. (2004)

Implications for Our School:
Questions for Discussion and Reflection

- How do we typically evaluate our school's programs and practices? Does the process need to be more organized?

- When we initiate a new program, do we talk about how it will be evaluated and what data will be needed for the evaluation?

- Do we use the results of evaluations to help us improve programs or make decisions about eliminating programs?

Follow-up and Action Items

_____

_____

_____

_____

_____

_____

_____

_____

_____

_____

_____

_____

_____

_____

_____

_____

_____

_____

Chapter 5

Using Assessment Data to Improve Instruction

> "Assessment is the process of gathering information about children
> from several forms of evidence, then organizing and interpreting that
> information." (McAfee, Leong, & Bodrova, 2004, p. 3)

Although much of the current emphasis on using assessment data began with data from high-stakes tests, schools that are the most effective users of assessment data have begun to recognize and capitalize on the power of classroom assessment. Damian urges teachers and school leaders to embed assessment in "every aspect of our planning, thinking, and doing" instead of viewing assessment as a "once-a-year crisis" (2000, p. 16). Gregory and Kuzmich talk about this more comprehensive approach:

> High-stakes test data gives us only one piece of evidence about student learning. Well-designed classroom data collection and analysis, the everyday information a teacher collects, form the backbone of student growth.... Effective use of classroom data increases the probability that more students will demonstrate proficient and higher levels of performance. (2004, pp. 9-10)

They go on to talk about diagnostic teaching, an approach built around data use. In their view, diagnostic teaching moves past simply assessing to gauge progress—or lack of it. Instead, "true diagnostic thinking requires teachers to reflect consciously on student learning and then connect their conclusions to the most effective next steps" (p. 52). Teachers using this type of diagnosis as a tool to improve their teaching collect data that allow them to answer these questions:

- What do I know about my students now?
- What is the nature and content of the final assessment for this unit or period of time?
- What don't I know about the content knowledge, the critical thinking, and the process or skill demonstration of my students? (Gregory & Kuzmich, 2004, p. 56)

Creating appropriate assessments and then using the data they produce takes time, time teachers often view as taken from instructional time they are reluctant to give up. Assessment, however, should be considered part of the teaching process and, when used effectively, can make teaching more productive and time-efficient. Recognizing this, effective teachers incorporate assessment opportunities into their lesson planning (Aschbacher, Koency, & Schacter, 1995). Sindelar describes a well-constructed data-driven instructional system as a "cyclical and recursive process" (2011, p. 33). In other words, results from both summative and formative assessments are used to inform the process of evaluating and possibly revising curriculum and instruction as well as assessing the progress of students.

"If you can't measure learning, you can't manage it. Improvement is left to chance, and a child's education is too important to leave to chance. If we can measure what an individual child knows and doesn't know, then we can provide the instruction he needs. We can manage it. We can improve." (Brett Gies, who worked as a principal, director of data analysis and program improvement, and superintendent, in Cawelti & Protheroe, 2001, p. 50)

An Assessment Framework

The heart of assessment is a continuing process in which both teachers and students use information to guide the next steps in learning. For the student, assessment provides feedback on understanding. Results of a test or comments on a written assignment will help him or her answer questions such as, "Am I getting it?" and, "How am I doing?" Assessments can help teachers answer related questions such as, "Which students are learning?" Similarly, an analysis of the results can help a teacher pinpoint a specific student's difficulties or misconceptions that need to be addressed. When applied to the class, the data can answer such questions as, "Is the class ready for a new unit?" Reviewing assessment information also helps a teacher decide who needs additional help—and what type of help—as well as who can move on.

There are specific characteristics that tell us that assessment is being effectively used to guide instruction in the classroom:

- Assessment is embedded and ongoing and provides prompt user-friendly feedback so adjustments can be made in a timely fashion.
- Day-to-day classroom assessments emphasize formative assessments—information that provides early indications of whether or not learning is taking place—to minimize problems that might arise if learning barriers are not promptly identified and addressed.
- Day-to-day classroom assessments include qualitative data such as information from classroom observation as well as quantitative measures.
- Students are told the purpose of an assessment and how this information will be used.

Niyogi highlights some elements of high-quality, classroom-based assessment that makes it a potentially powerful tool:

Assessment should be used not simply to judge how much kids know but to illuminate the nature of their knowledge and understandings in order to help kids learn.... Common sense tells us that ongoing, classroom-based assessment can serve this purpose. Teachers interacting with students will observe the nuances of their cognitive growth and development over time, their individual strengths and weaknesses in ways that would be extremely difficult, if not impossible, to capture through standardized or conventional testing alone. (1995, p. 3)

There are two broad types of assessment teachers can use to support instruction. First is formative assessment that provides both immediate feedback to students and information to help a teacher keep instruction on track. Examples of formative assessments include such things as practice tests or in-class question-and-answer sessions. Marshall calls such approaches "in-the-moment assessments" (2008, p. 66). In his view, "it makes perfect sense that these in-the-moment assessments improve teaching" and goes on to describe examples of elements in an in-the-moment "toolbox":

> students writing answers on small whiteboards and holding them up so the teacher can gauge the overall level of understanding; "clickers" that gather instant electronic data on in-class quizzes; journal writing and exit cards to give teachers quick feedback on what students understand; more effective teacher questioning; and methods that randomize which students are called on (e.g., pulling popsicle sticks out of a can, each one with a student's name written on it. (p. 66)

Formative assessments should be carefully planned to address two goals. The first goal is to accurately assess student learning and so provide direction for instruction. A variety of traditional methods can be used, ranging from multiple-choice tests, written assignments, and projects, as well as nontraditional methods such as games and panel discussions. Another method is to have the students maintain journals that teachers periodically review to provide additional information on individual and class progress.

Test questions and activities for formative assessments should parallel those of the summative assessment. However, the two should not be identical. For example, a math teacher teaching students how to solve a time/distance problem could create several parallel problems. The task is to teach the student how to solve the problem, not how to simply substitute one set of time-and-distance data for another.

The second goal of formative assessments is to provide meaningful feedback to students. One approach might be to discuss the items on a test. This discussion goes beyond simply giving the correct answer to also providing information on why the answer is correct and why others are incorrect. Research evidence shows that high-quality, formative assessment can have a powerful impact on student learning. Black and Wiliam report that studies of formative assessment show an effect size on standardized tests of between 0.4 and 0.7, larger than most known educational interventions (1998).

Marshall (2008) differentiates in-the-moment assessments from another type of formative assessment many schools use—interim assessments. He see these interim assessments as providing a more formal structure for assessing student learning and feels that schools should use both approaches.

In contrast to formative assessments, summative assessments are snapshots of a point in time of a student's learning. They should also carefully consider the type of feedback they provide to students. Feedback on a summative assessment varies depending on the type of assessment. A standardized test often only provides a score as feedback. However, a teacher-developed summative assessment should provide the same opportunities for feedback to students as a formative assessment.

The Potential Ripple Effect of Interim Assessments

Effective interim assessments can:

- Give teachers timely insights on the kinds of minute-by-minute classroom assessments that might nip student misconceptions and misunderstandings in the bud and prevent them from continuing week after week.

- Give teachers periodic feedback on whether their students are actually learning what's being taught—on what's working and what isn't working in the way they are orchestrating learning experiences.

- Give teachers feedback on ways to improve their unit and lesson planning for better student understanding and retention.

- Provide fine-grained data for teacher teams to analyze student learning results and plan improvements. These meetings are critical to improving teaching and learning and accelerating student achievement during the year.

- Identify students who need follow-up and the areas in which they need extra help; this could include skills and concepts that need to be re-taught to the whole class, to small groups, or to individual students [as well as provide] information for tutors and after school programs.

- Contribute to far better results on summative assessments without resorting to the "junk food" of test prep.

In short, effective use of interim assessments helps principals see the *results* of what teachers do in classrooms rather than looking only at the *process* of instruction. (Marshall, 2006a, p. 18)

What Are We Looking For?

Thus far in this chapter, we have hardly used the word data. But, obviously, generating data is the point of assessment. Data become the knowledge we need to improve instruction through the questions we ask when framing our analysis of the data—data from state assessments, data from end-of-unit tests, or even the type of data a teacher is constantly collecting when she watches students' faces for signs of understanding or confusion during a lesson.

At the teacher level, there are questions that should be asked continuously; for example,

- Are my teaching strategies working?
- What does this class need help with? What does this particular student need help with?
- What do students understand and what can they apply?
- What misconceptions do my students have? (North Carolina Department of Public Instruction, 1999)

"Challenging as it is, using data to improve teaching and learning is possible. In our experience, the key lies in building a school culture in which faculty members collaborate regularly and make instructional decisions based on evidence about students' skills and understanding." (Boudett & Steele, 2007, p. 2)

How Will We Look For It?

On a very basic level, teachers use data to identify ways to improve instruction. The first step is developing a plan—sometimes simply a mental framework—for organizing the data around important issues. One district has developed a structured process to help teachers focus on data questions and then to reflect on the answers as they strengthen their own use of instructional strategies (see Figure 5.1).

Teacher use of data is supported by another element of this district's plan. Teachers are provided with time to talk about student work—again using a structured process. Teachers in all schools meet one day a month to evaluate results from a range of student assessments and to plan instruction based on the results. Principals create teams of 3 to 4 teachers, with each of the teams working together for the entire school year.

The classroom goals protocol developed by district staff developers and pilot teams of teachers is used to structure work of the teams:

> Prior to each month's meeting, each teacher prepares by selecting an area where students are struggling. The teacher collects student work, either a formative or common summative assessment that demonstrates where students are having difficulty. The teacher then uses the protocol's forms to prepare a brief analysis of students' performance and to outline the lesson focus and assessment task for

Figure 5.1. Papillion-La Vista Schools: Applying Assessment Data to Instructional Improvement

Classroom Goal: Background Information

- What was the objective of the unit of study?
- What assessment method did you use?
- What strategies did you use to teach the objective?
- Based on the results of the assessment, what are the strengths of the students?
- Based on the results of the assessment, what are the weaknesses of the students?

Classroom Goal: Action Plan

SMART goals are specific, measurable, attainable, results-oriented, and time-bound. Example: My students will improve in writing in the traits of ideas and content as measured on the 6-trait scoring guide by the end of the first semester.

- My Classroom Goal (written as a SMART Goal).
- Instructional strategies or classroom activities I will use with my students.
- Describe the feedback you will give to students. *(For example: Will you provide specific and corrective feedback from a scoring guide? What will students do as a result of the feedback? Will students get feedback from other students?)*

Classroom Goal: Action Plan Follow-up
(attach to original Classroom Goal Action Plan)

- Since the last Classroom Goals meeting, I implemented the following instructional strategies or classroom activities.
- Describe the feedback you gave to students. *(For example: Did you provide specific and corrective feedback from a scoring guide? What did students do as a result of the feedback? Did students get feedback from other students?)*
- Instructional strategies or classroom activities I will use before the next meeting.

(Papillion-La Vista Schools, Nebraska. Information provided by Superintendent Jef Johnston).

background to share with the team. In addition to the completed form, teachers bring six samples of student work, representing two high-scoring students, two average-scoring students, and two low-scoring students. During the meeting, the team focuses on three questions:

1. Did your assessment match your instructional strategies?
2. What were student strengths?
3. What were student weaknesses? (Johnston, Knight, & Miller, 2007, p. 16)

During discussion, other teachers on the team suggest instructional strategies intended to address the area of concern. The teacher tries some of the suggested strategies, gathers data related to their impact, and returns to the group for more discussion the next month. The small size of the teams provides times for each of its members to discuss issues in depth.

In addition to these monthly "classroom goals" meetings, other teams in the elementary schools meet weekly to focus on: 1) curriculum planning and classroom assessment and 2) student interventions. Most elementary principals provide the time for these weekly 40-minute sessions by having teachers work together for 30 minutes before students arrive supplemented by 10-15 minutes during which other staff members—such as the literacy coach—lead short learning activities for students (Johnston et al., 2007).

As the example above illustrates, schools and districts are finding that increasing the time and opportunities teachers have to review and discuss student work together can have positive impact on efforts to strengthen instruction. Another example of a way to structure teacher collaboration around analysis of student work—around data—is provided below.

The Tuning Protocol

The Tuning Protocol developed by the Coalition of Essential Schools is a structured, facilitated conversation that involves a group of teachers (and sometimes others) in examining samples of student work to address a focusing question—usually about instructional practice or the quality of student work. It is often used as a way to address questions of goals or standards for an individual classroom or school.

A typical tuning protocol session brings together a group of teachers (10-15) with a facilitator who may come from outside or inside the school. One teacher (or a team of teachers) presents sample student work and the context for the work (the assignment or assessment rubric). The protocol follows a schedule calling for presentation of the task or project, clarifying questions, examination of student work samples, "warm" and "cool" feedback to presenting teacher(s), reflection by the presenting teacher, and debriefing of the process. The entire protocol takes about an hour and 15 minutes.

The protocol may be used as a "one-shot" instrument for addressing an important schoolwide question or issue or, probably more effectively, as part of ongoing professional development or planning. The Tuning Protocol also can be modified for use in classrooms as a teacher peer review tool.

Guidelines for Looking at Student Work

The following guidelines were developed by the Philadelphia Education Fund to help teacher teams get started with a process of inquiry. These guidelines were informed by the work of a variety of education organizations and practitioners.

1. Gather a team, or small group, of teachers together.

2. Select a piece of student work. The sample should demonstrate a rich variety of student learning. It can be a work-in-progress, a final piece, or a document of a performance. Also collect the scoring guide or rubric used to assess that piece. Make copies for team members, if possible.

3. If someone in the group is not familiar with your unit of study, take a few minutes to introduce its overall purpose, the activities that have been conducted, and the work that has been generated.

4. Discuss and write down one standard from... (those) that you expected students to address in this activity. What did you expect the students to know and be able to do?

5. Next, take a few minutes to look at the work as a group. Either read it aloud, or let each person take a turn looking at it.

6. Write down the group's observations about the work. Then write down comments and questions. You might allow each team member to do this first individually and then share in turn.

7. Next, use your scoring guide or rubric to assess the piece of work. If you do not yet have a scoring guide, re-read the standard you have identified and assess the work based on its criteria. (You might put together an informal rubric by doing this.)

8. Take a few minutes to discuss as a team the following questions: What can you see from your observations, comments, and questions that will help you assess student learning? How might these observations determine your next steps as a teacher? Do these observations tell you anything new about your unit of study or classroom activities? (Excerpted from Philadelphia Education Fund, n.d.b.)

How Will We Use the Data?

Data from assessments, whether formative or summative, should be examined from a variety of perspectives. Teachers should be looking for indicators—for patterns—in the data so that they can make the necessary classroom or learning accommodations for the class as a whole or for individual students.

This is another stage at which we need to ask questions to help discover meaning in the data. And again, it is important to ask the "right" questions. Asking *which* students are *not* meeting standards in reading as well as *how many* students are meeting standards provide two different data points, both of which may be important to identifying needed adjustments to instruction. Examples of useful questions may be:

- How often did the students demonstrate …?
- How did different children (or teams) differ on …?
- Which students/teams did …? How well?
- Where are the gaps? What was disappointing?
- What worked?
- What different approaches can I use to address a learning gap?
- Where do I/we need to change and improve?
- What strategies are most apt to support increased student learning?
- Which strategies need to be abandoned as ineffective?

The next step is an action step that takes answers to questions such as these and puts into place changes—sometimes little tweaks, sometimes large shifts—intended to improve instruction for an entire class or for one child. Some of these changes may happen in the classroom. Other times, a student may need additional supports outside the scope of his or her regular classroom.

> "The volume of things to teach is limitless, but the time to teach them is finite. Instructional time is probably our most valuable resource; we cannot afford to use it unwisely. By using data, diagnostic assessment, and disaggregation techniques, teachers and school principals can maximize the use of instructional time." (Downey, Steffy, Poston, & English, 2009, p. 63)

Your Role as Principal

Meyers and Rust stress the importance of helping teachers learn how to "assess their own work and its impact on their students" (2000, p. 34). To be successful, school leaders need to engage in conversations with teachers, using assessment data to diagnose strengths as well as areas in which the teachers need to modify their instruction. In addition, by providing teachers with time and opportunity for discussion that uses assessment data as a springboard, principals can strengthen a school's instructional program.

Implications for Our School: Questions for Discussion and Reflection

- Are all teachers in the school using data from formative assessments to routinely assess and adjust instruction? If not, what is needed to move us in this direction?

- Is time available for teachers to discuss approaches to formative assessment that have proved effective in their classrooms—or to visit each others' classrooms to observe innovative approaches?

- Are opportunities available for cross-grade discussion focused on data from assessments? If not, what would be a good first topic for discussion?

Follow-up and Action Items

_____

_____

_____

_____

_____

_____

_____

_____

_____

_____

_____

_____

_____

_____

Chapter 6

Response to Intervention (RTI) and Data Use

"Response to intervention is a dynamic problem-solving process in which data are integral in making decisions about what skills struggling readers lack, and whether intervention instruction provided has been effective." (Hall, 2008, p. 17)

Viewed from the perspective of broad goals, Response to Intervention (RTI) is intended to ensure that low-performing students receive support in a timely manner. Procedures embedded in RTI:

> begin by ensuring that the general education classroom is providing effective instruction and assessment for all students. RTI then offers a way to bridge gaps between general and special education services by providing scientifically based interventions quickly and efficiently for all students who need support, before going through a lengthy process to determine eligibility for special education. (Brown-Chidsey, 2007)

In a jointly issued white paper, the National Association of State Directors of Special Education and Council of Administrators of Special Education describe RTI as "the practice of providing high-quality instruction and interventions matched to student need, monitoring progress frequently to make decisions about changes in instruction or goals, and applying child response data to important educational decisions" (2006 p. 2).

> "For years, schools and teachers have been urged to become more data-driven—that is, to use student performance and other data to guide decisions about instructional programs and school improvement efforts.
>
> The reality is that statewide assessments drive most accountability systems, and it often takes months before schools and teachers receive this achievement data. By then, students have already moved into different classrooms, if not different schools. While the data may still be informative, using it to make decisions about a new group of students can be a little like trying to steer a car by looking through the rear-view mirror.
>
> One way for educators to make data-driven decisions in real time is to apply the principles of Response to Intervention (RtI), an early intervention model that targets students who are falling behind, allowing schools and teachers to move quickly to close learning gaps."
> (Apthorp, 2007, p. 8)

Walser characterizes it as "at once simple and complex" (2007). She goes on to talk about its use in one elementary school:

Four years ago, Callender's school, the Haggerty School in Cambridge, Mass., began a new approach to reading instruction when it received a federal Reading First grant... All K–3 students in the school are tested for critical pre-reading and reading skills in the fall, winter, and spring. Students who score in the "some risk" or "at risk" categories are scheduled for intensive interventions to help them catch up. Student progress is recorded on graphs and discussed in monthly meetings. Depending on the results, children may be reassigned to different groups for different kinds of interventions, with schedules changing accordingly.

Despite the complicated logistics, Callender says the new approach is worth it. "Before, there was only one plan all year, no matter what," the 17-year veteran recalls. "In June there would always be four to five kids who hadn't made the kind of progress I knew they could. I wondered, why am I always missing this same 20%?"

What was missing were alternatives for these children. At some point in the day, Callender's ten troubled readers will be pulled out of the class to work one-on-one with a specialist or in small groups for more reading practice. Some have learning disabilities, some don't. With RTI, Callender says, there are no more end-of-the-year surprises. (Walser, 2007)

While the initial emphasis of RTI is on successfully addressing the instructional needs of as many students as possible in the regular classroom—and without going through the process of establishing eligibility for special education before students can receive more intensive instruction, some students will need special education services. However, RTI can help with this process as well, as "it can provide schools with much-needed help to better distinguish between the truly disabled and those who might seem to need special education, but who really don't" (Fuchs in Walser, 2007).

Components of RTI

- Clear academic and behavioral benchmarks, system-wide screening, and early assessment to identify students at risk of not making benchmarks

- Problem identification by teams of teachers using multiple data sources to identify why a student may not be making benchmarks

- Tiered, research-based interventions starting with general education instruction and moving toward instruction that is more systematic and explicit, occurs more frequently or lasts longer, and occurs in smaller groups with the most effective teachers

- Monitoring and analysis of the student's progress to determine impact of the current intervention on student learning

- Use of data to support decisions concerning continuation of an instructional approach/intervention or introduction of a different approach (Apthorp, 2007).

Many of the key features of RTI have been in use in schools for over two decades. Educators may recognize both the features and names, such as Pre-Referral Intervention Model, Mainstream Assistance Team Model, School-Based Consultation Team Model, and Problem-Solving Model (Horowitz, 2005). However, the model has become much more refined, very data-driven, and has "entered the mainstream" (Walser, 2007).

How Does RTI Differ From Prereferral and Building Assistance Teams?

"RTI is a more comprehensive framework for providing instruction, related interventions, and targeted special education for students at risk . . . RTI is a schoolwide process for bringing stronger alignment to the instruction and assessment practices of a school and is generally more proactive and comprehensive than the more reactive and individualized functions of prereferral and child study teams." (Mellard & Johnson, 2008, p. 139)

Walser talks about reasons behind RTI's swift and substantial movement into schools across the country. First, it was specifically included as a strategy in the Reading First section of NCLB. Then, it "got another boost from the federal government in final regulations issued for the 2004 IDEA, the law governing special education":

Though the new IDEA regulations fall short of mandating RTI as a method for identifying children with learning disabilities, they say that states "cannot require" the use of IQ tests to diagnose learning disabilities and they permit states to use "alternate methods" such as RTI to identify learning disabilities. To support early intervention, the regulations allow up to 15% of federal special education funds to be used for this purpose in general education classrooms. (Walser, 2007)

While RTI has been given special status by IDEA, "RTI is not a special education process but a general education initiative that fits within school improvement efforts" (Canter, Klotz, & Cowan, 2008, p. 12). Therefore, school efforts to implement the process require close collaboration among regular and special education teachers.

Data Use and RTI

Data use is at the core of the RTI process, since RTI emphasizes "prevention and swift, data-driven intervention as soon as student difficulties are detected" (Martinez & Nellis, 2008, p. 146). This short overview from the North Dakota Department of Public Instruction Web site identifies some key connections between RTI and data use:

Data-based decision making is infused in all components of an RTI practice. At the screening level, data would be used to make decisions about which students are at risk of their needs not being met. In the progress monitoring stage, data are used to make decisions about effectiveness of interventions. Decisions to increase or decrease levels of intervention within a Tiered Service Delivery Model are based on student performance data. Data are also used to make decisions regarding the fidelity of implementation. (North Dakota Department of Public Instruction, n.d.)

Brown-Chidsey describes the tier-based system of educational services on which RTI is built:

- Tier 1 includes universal instruction and assessment of all students—in other words, the general education curriculum. Schools need to ensure that this instruction and assessment are research based and effective in helping students gain academic proficiency. Success at Tier 1 is defined as the student demonstrating at least the levels of knowledge and skill expected for his or her age and grade.

- Tier 2 includes selected instructional activities and assessments for students who have not achieved at the expected level while participating in Tier 1. An example of Tier 2 intervention is providing 30 minutes a day of additional reading or math instruction to first grade students who have not met grade-level benchmarks. Students receiving Tier 2 support are monitored weekly to learn whether their skills are improving. If their assessment data indicate progress, the students gradually receive less support until they are able to succeed within the general education (Tier 1) program. If they do not make progress after a specified period of Tier 2 instruction, the school either adjusts the students' Tier 2 instruction or refers them to Tier 3.

- Only at Tier 3 does the school take steps to determine whether a student has a disability that requires special education. At this stage, the school conducts a comprehensive evaluation of the student's skills, including the data obtained in Tiers 1 and 2, to determine why a student's performance is significantly different from that of other students of his or her age and grade and to decide what additional instructional supports the student needs. (Brown-Chidsey, 2007)

In addition, Brown-Chidsey provides a graphic representation of these tiers and of the prominent role data use plays in the system (see Figure 6.1).

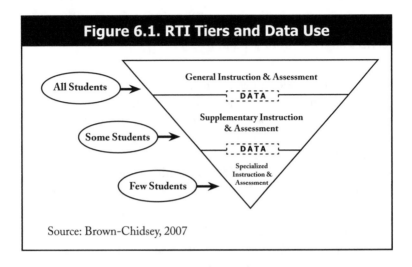

Figure 6.1. RTI Tiers and Data Use

General Instruction & Assessment

All Students

DATA

Supplementary Instruction & Assessment

Some Students

DATA

Specialized Instruction & Assessment

Few Students

Source: Brown-Chidsey, 2007

RTI *is* an approach for redesigning and establishing teaching and learning environments that are effective, efficient, relevant, and durable for all students, families, and educators.

RTI is *not*:
- A program, curriculum, strategy, or intervention
- Limited to special education
- New (Sugai, 2007)

What Are We Looking For?

The "What Are We Looking For?" question in regard to RTI is both very simple and very complex. It is simple because what you will be looking for are: 1) indicators that students are not succeeding and 2) reasons for this lack of success. It is complex because the reasons, in particular, may be difficult to identify. Sometimes, then, the RTI process will move forward by making some educated guesses about what the problem might be and what instructional strategies or supports might help to address this problem.

However, RTI has "guidelines" intended to guard against getting too far off base with these guesses. Specifically, the systematic and frequent reassessment of students receiving differentiated supports provide early indicators of whether the supports are—or are not—helping.

How Will We Look For It?

Data generation and analysis is at the core of RTI. Johnson, Mellard, Fuchs, and McKnight talk about approaches schools can use to collect data about "the status of students' knowledge, skills, and abilities" (2006). They categorize these into three broad groups: schoolwide screening, diagnostic tests, and progress monitoring procedures and highlight some distinguishing features of the three approaches (see Figure 6.2).

They then go on to talk in more detail about progress monitoring:

> Progress monitoring is a set of assessment procedures for determining the extent to which students are benefiting from classroom instruction and for monitoring effectiveness of curriculum. A fundamental assumption of education is that students will benefit from high-quality instruction. That is, typically, students will learn and achieve the skills and content taught in the classroom. For students who are not responsive to classroom instruction, alternative interventions can be provided and again the students'

response to that instruction can be monitored. Progress monitoring is a valid and efficient tool for gauging the effectiveness of instruction, determining whether instructional modifications are necessary, and providing important information for eventual classification and placement decisions. (Johnson et al., 2006)

Figure 6.2. Purposes of Three Types of Assessment

	Screening	Progress Monitoring	Diagnostic Tests
Population	Schoolwide	Class/small group/student	Individual student
Uses	Broad Index	Specific academic skill or behavioral target	Specific academic domains of knowledge, skills, or abilities
Frequency	Yearly/3X/ monthly	$\leq$ 3 weeks/ weekly/daily	Yearly
Purpose	Identify students who are at risk	Regroup students	Identify specific student deficits
Focus	School focus	Student/class focus	Student focus
Instruction	Class/school instruction and curriculum decisions	Within intervention (curriculum/ instruction)	Selecting curriculum and instructional methods
Implications	As first step for intervention planning	Continue to revise placement	Planning or specifying intervention

Source: Johnson et al., 2006

"Progress monitoring data inform decisions about when to adjust instruction, when to stay the course, and when to exit a student from intervention." (Hall, 2008, p. 29)

Hall states: "Why is progress monitoring so important? It is the heart of RTI. These are the data that are used to make adjustments in instruction along the way" (Hall, 2008, p. 82). Curriculum-based measurement (CBM) is considered "the formative assessment method of choice" (Martinez & Nellis, 2008, p. 151). However, other methods can be used to monitor student progress. The Vaughn Gross Center for Reading and Language Arts suggests that educators take the following purposes for progress monitoring into account when selecting approaches; progress monitoring should:

- assess the specific skills embodied in state and local academic standards
- assess marker variables that have been demonstrated to lead to the ultimate instructional target
- be sensitive to small increments of growth over time
- be administered efficiently over short periods
- be administered repeatedly (using multiple forms)
- result in data that can be summarized in teacher-friendly data displays
- be comparable across students
- be applicable for monitoring an individual student's progress over time
- be relevant to development of instructional strategies and use of appropriate curriculum that addresses the area of need. (2007, p. 4)

Tier 1:
Schoolwide Instruction and Student Assessment

In RTI, the continuum of services includes universal interventions at Tier 1, sometimes referred to as "primary prevention," which are in place for all students to support positive academic, behavioral, and mental health outcomes. Tier 1 in RTI involves a high-quality school and classroom environment, scientifically sound core curriculum and instruction, and intentional instructional practices. In Tier 1, school personnel must objectively and systematically evaluate whether their core curriculum materials are of sufficient quality and are backed by research. School staff must also evaluate teachers' instructional methods to make sure their teaching techniques adhere to sound instructional practice and are delivered as intended by the curriculum or intervention program.

To verify whether students are making adequate progress toward basic academic goals, it is imperative to gather data on the population. In Tier 1, schoolwide assessments are conducted to gauge students' performance in the core academic areas (e.g., reading and mathematics). All students are typically assessed three times per year (e.g., fall, winter, and spring) beginning in kindergarten. The purpose of conducting schoolwide assessments is to gather critical data about all students and to identify individuals and groups who are not making satisfactory progress and are at risk for academic or behavioral problems. Students who are not mastering basic academic skills may require additional or different forms of instruction. Systematic reviews of assessment data are often carried out by collaborative instructional support teams, which usually consist of a multidisciplinary team of school personnel such as general and special education teachers, principal, school counselor, school psychologist, and other related services personnel.

Tier 2:
Supplementary Instruction and Progress Monitoring

Tier 2, referred to as "secondary prevention," includes targeted academic and behavioral services for students who are considered at risk and for whom universal instruction was not sufficient. These students were flagged as being at-risk through the assessment process. Services at Tier 2 are more intense and are focused on the specific needs of a student or group of students. Examples of services at this second tier might include small group instruction for either academic or behavioral needs, additional support, and involvement in remediation programs such as Title I. Tier 2 interventions are provided to students in addition to the core curriculum.

In addition to the implementation of more targeted, systematic interventions at Tier 2, student progress at Tier 2 is monitored more frequently than it is at Tier 1 (often weekly) to determine student responsiveness to the interventions provided. Typically, those students who respond well to Tier 2 interventions and whose data demonstrate that they are progressing at an acceptable rate (e.g., above the 16th percentile) return to the general education curriculum or intervention offered to all students, or Tier 1. These students continue to participate in the assessment process.

Tier 3:
Intensive Instruction and Continued Progress Monitoring

Despite best efforts in the activities and assessments given at Tiers 1 and 2, some students will continue to struggle. More intensive services may be warranted. The intervention-assessment sequence in Tier 3 is markedly more intensive and individualized, and progress is monitored more frequently than it is in Tier 2. Current best practice in the field suggests that students who do not make adequate progress at Tiers 2-3 be further evaluated to rule out conditions such mental retardation and emotional disturbance. Persistent failure to make academic gains at Tiers 2-3 may substantiate the presence of a learning disability.

Excerpted from Martínez, Nellis, & Prendergast, 2006

Why RTI Works

- The strategies and tools are systematic.
- The process is data driven.
- It is based on scientific research and evidence-based solutions.
- It demands problem solving and collaboration.
- It creates solutions to identified problems. (Arnberger & Shoop, 2008, p. 54)

How Will We Use the Data?

Obviously, data collection and use under the RTI framework is not a one-time process. School staff members will need to analyze and apply the data to decision making frequently. Establishing a systematic approach to this is important. The National Association of State Directors of Special Education and Council of Administrators of Special Education suggest that:

> the use of a structured, problem-solving process is a requisite component of RTI. A structured, systematic problem-solving process assists in the identification of student learning needs and has some basic components. These components include problem identification, analysis of the problem to hypothesize why it is occurring, developing a plan to address the problem, and evaluating the student's response to the intervention/plan selected. (2006, p. 5)

It might be helpful to use a practical perspective to frame staff discussion about RTI. For example, the National Center for Learning Disabilities tells educators to:

think of RTI as a series of steps. The first step is instruction in the general classroom. Screening tests given in the classroom reveal students at risk for reading and other learning difficulties. For example, testing may show that a student who has difficulty reading needs additional instruction in phonics.

In the second step, the classroom teacher might handle the instruction. In other cases, someone who has expertise in reading and phonics might instruct the student and other students who have the same difficulty.

Students who fail to respond to this instruction may then be considered for more specialized instruction in step three, where instruction may occur with greater frequency or duration. If the achievement difficulties persist, a team of educators from different fields (for example, reading or counseling) may complete a comprehensive evaluation to determine eligibility for special education and related services. (National Center for Learning Disabilities, n.d.)

The challenge for school staff members is to identify both the "step" at which a student should be placed and instructional strategies that, when used in that setting, can help the student achieve success. The process is also cyclical, with staff members stepping back periodically to review new assessment results to see whether the "right" approach has been selected (Linan-Thompson, Vaughn, Prater, & Cirino, 2006). Tweaking the approach or intentionally shifting to another one can be a next step if the student still fails to experience success.

Response to Intervention:
Using Data to Analyze Problems and
Look for Instructional Solutions

Analyze the Problem—Points to Consider: Look at the problem as the difference between what is expected and what occurs. Analyze the problem with respect to the characteristics of the environment, instruction, curriculum, and the individual learner. Other questions may include:

- Is the instruction delivered with fidelity?
- Is the student missing tool skills (alterable)?
- How is the information provided during instruction?
- What are the characteristics of the learning environment?
- How is the curriculum organized?
- What has not worked in the past?
- What has worked in the past?

Based on the data you have collected, why do you think the problem is occurring?

_____

_____

_____

_____

_____

_____

Develop a Plan

Goal: Write a meaningful, measurable, observable goal. Include the conditions (time frame, materials, setting), student's name, behavior, and criterion.

_____

_____

_____

_____

_____

_____

_____

Identify Potential Interventions: Generate a list of interventions. Evaluate each one keeping in mind the research base and record the top six. Place an asterisk (*) by the intervention methods(s) selected for implementation.

1. _____

2. _____

3. _____

4. _____

5. _____

6. _____

Source: Bergeson, Heuschel, Harmon, Gill, Alig, & Middling, 2006

"While data, graphs, assessment results, and effective tools all make up a substantial part of progress monitoring, the most significant piece is the classroom teacher. It is often said that data drive instruction. If that were true, there would be no need for progress monitoring—the data would select the appropriate instruction, and monitoring for growth would not be necessary. The truth is that the teachers drive the instruction while the data help to guide them." (Vaughn Gross Center for Reading and Language Arts, 2007, p. 4)

Horowitz talks about the use of data to monitor a student's status as part of the progress monitoring components of RTI:

Data are collected to document how well students respond to targeted instruction; this in turn guides decisions about how to adjust classroom instruction and whether a formal referral for special education assessment is warranted. (Horowitz, 2005)

In addition, IDEA now states that data from progress monitoring can also be used as an alternative to use of the "discrepancy model" to determine whether a student is eligible for special education services; specifically,

Schools are allowed to use evidence of a student's failure to respond to instructional interventions as part of the data documenting the presence of a specific learning disability. (Brown-Chidsey, 2007)

The Principal's Role

So far, the focus in this chapter has been on the details of the process of RTI and on the potential it has for improving all students' opportunities for educational success. However, it is important to recognize that the process will initially require more time, much collaboration, and generate some frustration when instructional approaches do not work. In addition, some teachers may initially experience discomfort with the process since it focuses in a very public way on students who are not experiencing success in their classrooms.

Dealing with all these aspects of RTI implementation—administrative details such as scheduling along with sometimes more difficult issues such as teacher confidence—will require leadership, patience, and, often, some creativity.

An educator interviewed as part of a National Research Center on Learning Disabilities (NRCLD) research project talked about his school's implementation of RTI:

> As we have implemented the RTI process it has continued to be an ongoing challenge at times with staff to have them understand their role and responsibility in the process. And so we continue to go back to data—having data drive our discussion so that we get the feeling side out and get the data side in to help them see that this is about helping the child—it's not evaluating whether they're a

good or bad instructor or that it's being perceived that way. But it's about finding the right match, for the right child to get the right intervention started. So, is it easy? No. Is it a long-term process? Yes. (National Research Center on Learning Disabilities, n.d.)

Finally, Hall suggests that you "build your base of support around RTI as the right thing to do, not the required thing to do" (Hall, 2008, p. 21).

Implications for Our School: Questions for Discussion and Reflection

- Review the questions in the "Analyze the Problem" section of the box on page 82. Regardless of whether your school is using a formal RTI process, are questions such as these used to collect data about a struggling student?

- If your school is currently implementing RTI, are there any problem areas? How could these be addressed?

- If your school is not currently implementing RTI but plans to do so, what are some potential roadblocks that will need to be addressed?

Follow-up and Action Items

_____

_____

_____

_____

_____

_____

_____

_____

_____

_____

_____

_____

_____

_____

_____

Chapter 7

Using Data to Reduce the Dropout Rate

"While there is no single pathway that every dropout follows, there are common patterns, common crisis spots in the pipeline and common signposts, too." (Jerald, 2006, p. 15)

O bviously, a goal for educators is to have students graduate from high school. We know this milestone can impact the rest of their lives as well as society as a whole. Students who graduate are more likely to be employed, to receive higher salaries, and will be less likely to need any types of social services.

However, NCLB regulations—especially the requirement that dropout data will be disaggregated in the same way that achievement scores have been—add extra emphasis to the focus schools and districts must place on providing supports for students at risk of dropping out. These regulations will put additional pressure on high schools and, quite probably, on elementary and middle schools as districts recognize that dropout prevention needs to be addressed well before high school.

What Does Research on Dropouts Tell Us?

Dropout research has been an increasingly hot topic for researchers and advocacy groups over the last few years, with attention given recently to synthesizing this body of research. For a school engaged in data-informed decision making, the information—the data—available through this research base provides a critically important starting point.

- No single factor can completely account for a student's decision to continue in school until graduation (Rumberger & Sun, 2008, p. 67). In addition, "even though a factor is related to dropout, it does not mean that it *causes* dropout" (Hammond, Smink, & Drew, 2007, p. 21).

- There might not be one single "leading indicator" that all dropouts exhibit first.... In other words, for many dropouts, "one thing can lead to another." But it is not always the *same* thing (Jerald, 2006, p. 16).

- Dropouts are not a homogeneous group. Some exhibit risk factors early in school, while others not until middle or high school. Factors do not influence all students in the same way—some may have multiple risk factors and not drop out while others have one factor and leave school early (Hammond et al., 2007, p. 21).

- There are two important categories of risk factors—low academic performance (for example, low grades or test scores, falling behind in required course credits, and retention in grade) and educational engagement (for example, high rates of truancy or absenteeism, disciplinary problems, low participation in extracurricular activities (Jerald, 2006).

- Dropping out is more of a process than an event. For many students, the process begins in early elementary school. A number of long-term studies that tracked groups of students from preschool or early elementary school through the end of high school were able to identify early indicators that could significantly predict whether students were likely to drop out or finish high school (Rumberger & Sun, 2008, p. 67).

- "Even though a student shares certain risk factors with other students who have dropped out, it doesn't mean that a *particular* student will drop out. In addition, no one factor stood out as a primary cause of dropout." (Hammond et al., 2007, p. 18)

- The accuracy of dropout predictions increases when *combinations* of multiple risk factors are considered (Hammond et al., p. 2).

- "Dropouts in a district can 'clump' into subgroups based on the grade level in which they leave school, and those subgroups can exhibit very different educational pathways to dropping out. For example, [Roderick] found that Fall River dropouts who left before 10th grade exhibited clear warning signs as early as 4th grade, but later dropouts showed their clearest warning signs during the transitions to middle school and high school" (Jerald, 2006, p. 16).

- The transition to middle school and high school is a critically important time for students. Many dropouts begin to show warning signs and downward trends in 6th grade or 9th grade. Transition-year failure often begins very early, and powerful risk factors can be observed even during the first month of school. Students with poor prior achievement and behavior are more likely to fail during transition years. However, it can be hard to predict transition-year failure based solely on information collected the year before students change schools (Jerald, 2006, p. 17). For example, research has found that students with low eighth-grade test scores are not automatically doomed to ninth-grade failure.

Jerald highlights a finding from the research base on factors associated with dropping out that is especially important for educators:

> The conventional wisdom that dropping out is a highly idiosyncratic process driven by entirely personal factors is not true for most students who leave school. Most dropouts follow identifiable pathways through the education pipeline.... We can do a much better job predicting which students are most likely to drop out. An ongoing study in Philadelphia can now identify half of all eventual high school dropouts as early as 6th grade. And a group of Chicago researchers can predict 85 percent of eventual dropouts in that city's public school system based on just a few facts about the system's 9th graders. (2006, p. 3)

Finally, Jerald also stresses that education-related factors—such as low grades or absenteeism—associated with high dropout rates should be given high levels of attention by educators:

> because they are *practical* and because they are *predictive*. First, such factors describe something that takes place inside of school rather than something that happens in the home or that students bring with them from outside. As such, they can be helpful in determining the kinds of interventions that students might need and that education systems can provide.
>
> Second, educational experiences can be powerful predictors of dropping out, either along with demographic factors or, in some kinds of communities, even apart from

them. Especially in urban districts, where high proportions of students have demographic risk factors, very low academic performance and educational engagement can help discriminate the ones most likely to be on the path to dropping out. (2006, pp. 5-6)

"As pressure mounts to do something about the dropout problem, many school systems will be tempted to skip questions about how to predict which students are most at risk of dropping out and simply begin with reforms meant to solve the problem. Leaders might assume that educators can do a pretty good job guessing which students are at risk based on subjective judgments. Or they might simply decide not to spend money on data systems but rather invest all of their dollars in interventions and reforms instead . . . [H]owever, such decisions can have a variety of negative consequences.

Indeed, the cost of building an accurate Early Warning System is relatively small compared with the cost of providing programmatic interventions or systemwide reforms meant to increase graduation rates. The payoff of basing interventions on accurate data can be huge." (Jerald, 2006, p. 3)

Schools and school districts have begun to recognize the importance of developing approaches for early identification of potential dropouts for two reasons—first, to increase the likelihood that these students receive the extra supports they need and, second, to make the allocation of scarce resources more cost-effective.

As an example of the second, it would not be cost-effective to provide services intended to address the dropout problem to all low-income children—although research has found such students are at higher risk of not graduating—since a high percentage of them *will* graduate *without* special supports. One North Carolina district analyzed data in an effort to identify predictors of students who would drop out in ninth grade. A composite of three factors—retention in grade in any year, long-term suspension in either eighth or ninth grade, and below grade level score on eighth grade end-of-course exam or failure in ninth grade algebra—was 84% successful in predicting a student's likelihood of dropping out. Although adding other factors could potentially have identified an additional 9%, the addition also created too many "false positives" and services would have been provided to students who didn't really need them (Sparks, Johnson, & Akos, 2008).

Findings From Specific Studies

While the information above represents a synthesis of research findings about dropouts and factors related to dropping out, Jerald highlights three well-designed studies that deserve special attention. They are especially interesting because each of the three focused on students at different points in their education and so could provide helpful guidance to educators in elementary, middle, or high schools.

Fall River Study

Jerald characterizes the study conducted by Roderick in the early 1990s in the Fall River, Massachusetts, school district as a "pioneering research project" (2006, p. 9). Roderick began her work with students enrolled in seventh grade and followed these students through the year in which they should have graduated.

Roderick (1994) found that 70% of the students who were retained a grade between kindergarten and eighth grade dropped out compared to 27% of those who did not repeat a grade. In addition, those who repeated and dropped out were more likely than students who didn't repeat but still dropped out to leave soon as soon as they legally could (at age 16).

Although this association between retention and dropout was strong, it was the additional analysis done by Roderick (1994) that provided even more illuminating data for educators, in particular her focus on grades and transition years. Jerald talks about her findings:

> First, she discovered comparing all dropouts to all graduates masks important variations among subgroups. At first, her analysis seemed to indicate that dropouts were immediately distinguishable by warning signs as early as the 4th grade. On average, 4th graders who would eventually drop out had substantially lower grades compared with their peers who would graduate. However, when she probed more deeply, Roderick discovered that the gap was being driven by two subgroups. The average 4th grade performance of dropouts was being pulled down by a subgroup of very low performers—about one-third of all dropouts—who would eventually drop out before even making it to 10th grade. The average 4th grade performance of graduates was being pulled up by a subgroup of high performers who would graduate in the top two-thirds of their class.

Second, her analysis revealed that the district had two very distinct types of dropouts—those who left school between 7th and 9th grades (early dropouts), and those who left during 10th through 12th grades (later dropouts). Not only did members of these two groups leave school at different points in the pipeline, they also had very different educational careers—exhibiting different risk factors at different points in time. Early dropouts started out with much lower grades in elementary school. However, later dropouts—who made up 65 percent of all Fall River dropouts—had 4th grade attendance and grades that looked no different from students who would eventually graduate in the bottom third of the class.

Third, Roderick uncovered powerful evidence that the transition years—during which students move from elementary to middle school and from middle to high school—had a decisive impact on students who would later drop out. During the transition to middle school, academic performance declined for nearly all students. But the deterioration was much steeper for students who eventually dropped out. The same thing happened later during the transition to high school.

In effect, the two transitions were like hurdles that some students tripped over, causing them to fall behind their peers in the trek to graduation. Even though their grades did not decline more than graduates' during the non-transition years, most dropouts never made up the ground they lost during 6th and 9th grades. (Jerald, 2006, pp. 9-10)

Consortium on Chicago School Research Study

This study by Allensworth and Easton (2007) tracked almost 25,000 ninth-graders in the Chicago public schools through the year they would have graduated. Freshman year data analyzed included:

- On-track status: A student was considered on-track if he or she had accumulated 10 semester credits and had no more than one semester F in a core subject (English, math, science, or social science) by the end of the first year in high school.
- Absence rates
- GPA
- Course failures

Project researchers were looking for indicators strongly associated with dropping out and also looked to see whether factors that could be observed prior to ninth grade, such as student socioeconomic status, had a strong predictive quality. They found:

Students' freshman-year course performance is much more important for graduation than their background characteristics and prior achievement. Graduation is related to students' gender, race, and economic status. However, all of these factors together explain only about 12 percent of the variation in graduation rates in the cohort of students.... [In contrast] ninth-grade Fs or GPA each can be used to predict about 80 percent of graduates. (Allensworth & Easton, 2007, p. 8)

A practical application of this research was the development of what the researchers called an "on-track indicator"—a composite of two ninth-grade data elements that were highly predictive of likelihood of graduation or dropout. Ninth-graders were classified as on track if they:

1. had no more than one F in one semester in a core course and
2. earned at least five full-year course credits.

This early indicator made it possible to provide interventions for students at high risk of dropping out before they were so far behind they—and, often, their schools—considered graduation an impossibility.

The researchers also found that other data can sometimes be used to identify with even higher degrees of likelihood the possibility that a student will drop out. For example,

> Among students with the same number of Fs, higher grades in other courses increase the likelihood of graduation…. [while] students who just barely pass their freshman classes are likely to struggle as they move into their sophomore year. (Allensworth & Easton, 2007, p. 10)

Philadelphia Study

Balfanz, Herzog, and Mac Iver analyzed data from almost 13,000 students enrolled in the Philadelphia Public Schools from sixth grade through one year beyond on-track high school graduation in an attempt to answer these questions:

Can we identify a set of indicators that flag sixth graders who have high odds of falling off the graduation track and do these indicators collectively flag a substantial percentage of the students who do not graduate with a high school diploma? (Balfanz, Herzog, & Mac Iver, 2006, p. 9)

The researchers also wanted to identify a "parsimonious" set of indicators that would be helpful to schools in a practical sense. They talk about this:

We looked to have a small set of indicators that were not overwhelming in complexity. For this reason, we decided that we wanted to emerge with a unique set of indicators, each with its own independent and additive predictive power rather than composites or indexes. We decided to set a 75% yield as our initial screening level. Could we find a set of predictive indicators that individually identified sixth-graders who had a 75% or more risk of not graduating from the school district? (Balfanz et al., 2006, p. 9)

Through their extensive analysis of data on "high yield predictors," the researchers were able to show that:

four simple factors—attending less then 80% of the time, receiving a poor final behavior grade, failing math, or failing English *in sixth grade* [emphasis added]—could identify close to half of the students who would ultimately fail to graduate from the school district. (Balfanz et al., 2006, p. 9)

While successful in answering their focus questions, Balfanz et al. characterized this as their most significant finding:

> Our results show that early manifestation of academic and behavioral problems at the start of the middle grades do not self-correct, at least within the context of middle grade schools that serve high-poverty populations. A common response to students who struggle in sixth grade is to wait and "hope they grow out of it," to attribute early struggles to the natural commotion of early adolescence and experiencing new organizational structures of schooling. Our evidence clearly indicates, that at least in high-poverty schools, students who are missing 20% or more school, receiving poor behavior marks or failing math or English in 6th grade do not recover. On the contrary, they drop out. This says that early intervention is not only productive but is absolutely essential. Without it, these students will not succeed. (2006, pp. 22-23)

"The key to raising graduation rates lies not just in identifying the best intervention strategies, but also in building powerful data systems that target the right services to the right students in the right schools at the right time. The good news is that we know much more about how to do that than ever before." (Peltzman & Jerald, 2006, p. 8)

What Are You Looking For?

It is clear from the research that the "what" question related to efforts to reduce the dropout rate is simultaneously simple and complex. Simple because it involves looking for indicators that a student—or a group of students—might be at higher-than-average risk of dropping out. And complex because addressing the question effectively requires looking for patterns in data that might begin well before a student reaches high school and that are typically made up of several interrelated indicators.

Let's pull out one slice of these indicators—socioeconomic status—to see what it tells us about the likelihood that a student will drop out. While, on the face of it, poor students as a group drop out at a significantly higher rate than more affluent students, researchers caution us that this is not the entire story. Significant percentages of poor children *do* graduate from high school, while many children from more affluent families do not.

Mishook et al. urge educators to focus on "leading indicators." They contrast these with "lagging indicators"—such as dropout statistics or end-of-year test scores—that "usually arrive too late to help individual children or schools that are struggling" (2008). Leading indicators are powerful resources since they are:

- **Timely and actionable:** They are reported with enough time to change a course of action in order to improve lagging outcomes.

- **Benchmarked:** Users understand what constitutes improvement on leading indicators, whether through longitudinal comparison of the same data or through research-based criteria.

- **Powerful and predictive:** They can offer targets for improvement and show progress—or a lack of progress— toward a desired outcome before that outcome can be expected to occur. (Mishook et al., 2008)

Most important from the perspective of educators working to increase the likelihood of positive outcomes for individual students, leading indicators:

> provide early signals of progress toward academic achievement [and] enable education leaders…to make more strategic and less reactive decisions about services and supports to improve student learning. (Mishook et al., 2008)

Thus, what you want to begin with is a search to identify leading indicators that seem to be linked—in *your* school or district—with high incidences of dropout. Although researchers have found that patterns may look different in some schools than in others, the research obviously provides a place to start.

Peltzman and Jerald (2006) talk about the importance of what they call a Phase I analysis of data to begin developing an understanding of what factors are strongly associated with dropping out. They have summarized research-based findings for: 1) middle and high schools and 2) three major categories of factors (social background, academic performance, and educational engagement). (See Figure 7.1.) They suggest that schools—or districts—begin their search for leading indicators with these data elements.

Figure 7.1. Top Priority Student-Level Data Elements to Use in a Phase 1 Analysis

	Social Background	Academic Performance	Educational Engagement

Middle School	1. SES—FRPL eligibility, family income, etc.
	2. Race/ethnicity
	3. Gender
	4. Mobility—number of schools enrolled
	5. Years overage for grade
		1. Grades in academic subjects including at least English and math by end of quarter, semester, and year
		2. Failing grades in math and English
		3. Scores on standardized assessments in at least reading and math, including grade-level and benchmark assessments
		4. Number of times retained in grade during elementary and middle schools
			1. Attendance—number of days or percentage of days absent
			2. Discipline problems—indicators of poor behavior, including, for example:
			  a) Classroom behavior marks;
			  b) Number of office referrals;
			  c) Number of counseling referrals; and,
			  d) Number of suspensions.
			3. Grades in nonacademic subjects such as art, music, and phys ed, aggregated into one score (Roderick, 1993)

High School	1. SES—FRPL eligibility, family income, etc.
	2. Race/ethnicity
	3. Gender
	4. Mobility—number of schools enrolled
	5. Years overage for grade
		1. Grades in core academic subjects, by end of quarter, semester, and year
		2. Number of courses failed and passed in core courses, by end of quarter, semester, and year
		3. Number of credits attempted by semester, by year, and cumulatively
		4. Number of credits earned by semester, by year, and cumulatively
		5. GPA by semester, by year, and cumulatively
		6. 9th grade "on track indicator" equivalent to or adapted from measure developed by Consortium on Chicago School Reform:
		  a) Earned enough credits to be promoted; and,
		  b) Received not more than one semester F in core academic subject, with same calculated for subsequent grade levels.
		7. On-time promotion to 10th grade
		8. Scores on standardized assessments, including grade-level, end-of-course, benchmark assessments, and exit exams
		9. Dropped out previously and re-enrolled
			1. Attendance—number of days or percentage of days absent
			2. Discipline problems—indicators of poor behavior, including, for example:
			  a) Number of office referrals;
			  b) Number of counseling referrals; and,
			  c) Number of suspensions.

NOTE: The numbering of data elements in this table is not meant to imply rank-ordering on the basis of priority. All elements in this table are high priority. The relative predictive power of any element will vary by location (Peltzman & Jerald 2006, p. 10).

Heppen and Therriault (2008) have also reviewed the research and have developed a more limited list of what they call "high-yield indicators" (2008, p. 2) since the needed data is all available during a student's freshman year (see Figure 7.2.). They go on to suggest that such elements of predictive data—once analysis of these factors in the school or district verifies a strong association between any of them and dropping out—should be used to create early warning systems that allow intervention when there is "still time to intervene" (2008, p. 2). In their view, such early warning

Figure 7.2. Summary of High-Yield Indicators

Type of Information	Indicator	Brief Description	Benchmark (Red Flag)
Attendance	Absenteeism rate	Number of days absent during the first 20 days and each quarter of the first year of high school	The equivalent of more than 10% of instructional time missed during the first year indicates student may be at risk.
Course Performance	Course failures	Number of Fs in any semester-long course during the first year of high school	Even one failed course indicates student may be at risk.
	Grade point average (GPA)	GPA for each semester and cumulative GPA	GPA under 2.0 indicates student may be at risk.
	On-track indicator	Combination of the number of Fs in **core** academic courses and credits earned during the first year of high school	Two or more Fs in core academic courses *and/or* fewer than one-fourth of the credits required to graduate minus one indicate that student is off track to graduate.

Source: Heppen & Therriault, 2008, p. 5.

systems should use *"routinely available* [emphasis added] data housed at the school that are predictors of whether a student is likely to drop out of high school" (2008, p. 2).

Figure 7.3. Exploring Possible Indicators

The goal is to identify the "highest yield" indicators for your school and district. For individual risk factors or combinations of factors, ask these four questions:

1. What percentage of students *with* each risk factor (or combination) dropped out?

2. What percentage of students *with* each risk factor (or combination) graduated in 4 (or 5) years?

3. What percentage of students *without* each risk factor (or combination) dropped out?

4. What percentage of students *without* each risk factor (or combination) graduated in 4 (or 5) years?

Questions 1 and 4 represent the accuracy or predictive validity of the risk factors. These high-yield indicators are those that predict which students will drop out.

Question 2 represents the "false negatives," and Question 3 represents the "false positives." The "high-yield" indicators for the district are those with as few of these as possible.

The results of these exploratory analyses of the "high-yield" indicators in the district should drive the creation of the early warning system. That is, not all of the student and school characteristics included in the exploratory dataset need to be incorporated into the early warning system—the effectiveness of the early warning system depends on the ease of data collection at the school level, and extraneous (i.e., non-"high yield") information should not be included. (Heppen & Therriault, 2008)

How Will You Look for It?

The "how will you look for it?" question in this chapter might actually be phase two of "what are you looking for?" Once your school or district has identified indicators that have an especially strong tie to students dropping out, collecting and analyzing individual student level data on these indicators should be a routine and ongoing process in your school.

There are tools available to help with this. For example, the National High School Center provides an online Early Warning System Tool into which high school leaders can enter a few key pieces of data. The tool—an Excel spreadsheet—"automatically calculates high-yield indicators related to dropout such as those involving attendance, course failures, GPA, and on-track status and provides a report that shows which students are below the defined benchmark on each of the indicators" (O'Cummings, Heppen, Therriault, Johnson, & Fryer, 2010).

Edwards and Edwards talk about an approach that requires teacher-level watchfulness. They suggest that students exhibiting problems in one or more areas—poor attendance, failure to complete homework, inadequate basic skills, or bad behavior—be identified by teachers after no more than 15 days. In their view,

> This 15-day benchmark is critical; if educators do not establish interventions early, it is likely that an entire quarter will lapse before aid is provided. Identifying problems with individual students early gives the school

and teachers adequate time to implement essential interventions that will keep kids in school. (Edwards & Edwards, 2007, p. 14)

How Will You Use the Data?

"Identifying students at risk of dropping out by using an early warning system is only the first step in addressing the dropout challenge" (Heppen & Therriault, 2008, p. 7). Next steps include:

- immediately providing intervention strategies for students identified most at risk, with these strategies tailored to meet the needs of the individual student (for example, help with a particular course needed for graduation vs. more general supports intended to address problems with academics);

- monitoring these students to gauge whether the impact of the interventions will likely be enough to help them through to graduation and changing/intensifying supports if necessary;

- also monitoring students who—while not thought to be at a critical level of risk—might still need extra help; and,

- attempting to identify and address schoolwide areas of concern that may be negatively affecting students in ways that make it more likely they will drop out (for example, suspension policies that create academic problems due to number of days a student is absent).

One elementary and one middle school in Philadelphia are piloting the Keeping Middle Grade Students on Track to Graduation approach that is built on research conducted in the district. A tiered plan of interventions has been developed for each of the Big Four risk factors— attending less than 80% of the time, receiving a poor final behavior grade, and failing math or English in sixth grade. The interventions are provided in accordance with the plan below:

- *Schoolwide* interventions are part of the daily whole-school and classroom programs. When planned and implemented effectively, whole-school interventions keep 70-80% of students on track. The remaining 20-30% of students require additional supports, either targeted or intensive.

- *Targeted* interventions, serving 10-20% of students, are defined as having a 1:15 to 1:20 adult-student ratio, with moderate levels of concentrated help from the teacher or program provider.

- *Intensive* interventions, serving up to 10% of students, are defined as having a maximum 1:5 adult-student ratio with high levels of concentrated help from the teacher or program provider. (Philadelphia Education Fund, n.d.a.)

Roderick used findings from her Fall River research project to support the need for specific interventions. For example, since she found that school transitions from elementary to middle school and from middle to high school were "critical junctures" (1993, p. 145) for students, she suggests that special supports for students already identified as being at risk were especially needed to help them make the adjustments.

After first identifying factors highly associated with a student's likelihood of dropping out in ninth grade, one school district used the data about these factors to better identify students who needed strong interventions—and quickly. Because the data also helped to narrow the group served to fewer students, high schools in the district were able to provide more and better targeted interventions to students most at risk (Sparks et al., 2008).

Graduation coaches in Georgia are trained to use a commonsense approach toward data analysis. They look at potential risk factors that had been identified as links to high incidence of dropout—for example, retention, absenteeism in the current or previous years, or lagging behind in credits earned. They then work to focus school efforts on intervention for students most at risk (Georgia Department of Education, 2006).

In Summary

While data use obviously cannot "do the work" students need to help them stay in school through graduation, it provides a critically important starting place. First, by using data to analyze patterns of behaviors, experiences, etc.—the leading indicators—of students who have already dropped out, your school and district can potentially identify some important links in the path to dropping out. Second, this knowledge can provide a foundation for discussions, planning, and action around developing targeted, cost-effective supports for the students most at risk. Third, data should be used in an ongoing way to assess the effectiveness of these supports in decreasing the numbers of students who drop out.

Implications for Our School: Questions for Discussion and Reflection

- Has our school intentionally used data to identify factors related to dropout behavior? If so, have we identified any high-yield indicators?

- Is our approach to providing interventions for students at risk of dropping out effective? If not, how can we improve on both the interventions used and the ways in which they are provided to students?

- Have there been conversations with staff at either feeder schools (if your school is a middle or high school) or with staff at schools to which you send students about ways to better identify and support these at-risk students through the grades?

Follow-up and Action Items

_____

_____

_____

_____

_____

_____

_____

_____

_____

_____

_____

_____

_____

_____

Chapter 8

Using Teacher Observation Data to Improve Instruction

> "Observing teachers as they practice their craft provides the most fundamental connection between the instructional leader's role in overseeing the educational program and the teacher's role in implementing that program." (Williams, Cray, Millen, & Protheroe, 2002, p. 20)

One of a principal's most important responsibilities is ensuring that quality teaching occurs in every classroom. Student performance on required end of the year assessments is one source of data about the quality of instruction. But waiting until the end of the year would mean many months of missed opportunities to help teachers improve their instructional skills. The once-a-year checklist observations of teachers used by many districts for evaluation purposes also suffer from the "too little, too late" problem.

More frequent and targeted classroom visits, on the other hand, can provide valuable information about what happens in classrooms on a day-to-day basis. When followed up by feedback to and conversations with teachers, principals have a powerful tool to improve instruction. Williams et al. view teacher observations as:

an essential means of enhancing the professional knowledge and skills of teachers and building their confidence
to meet the needs of diverse learners. Rather than single,
isolated events, teacher observations should be a regular
part of the professional working environment, seamlessly
integrated with the overall professional development process. (2002, p. 14)

They also provide a framework that contrasts what they call the
traditional and new paradigms of teacher observations and suggest that the new paradigm better addresses today's "challenges of
creating and sustaining a high-performing teaching and learning
environment" (p. 18). (See Figure 8.1)

The National Association of Elementary School Principals
(NAESP) recognizes the importance of teacher observation, as
well as the principal's responsibility for it:

Effective principals spend large amounts of time in classrooms, observing the teaching of academic units and provide detailed feedback regarding how teachers' effectiveness can be improved. The point of principal and peer
observations is not to catch a teacher doing something
wrong. The point is to ensure that all students are mean-
ingfully engaged, actively learning, and that teachers are
not simply presenting material.

An important part of classroom observations is to evaluate the instructional skills of individual teachers, to assist these teachers in improving those skills, and to help them grow professionally. Collaboration with other teachers and assignment of a mentor may be strategies a principal suggests to assist the teacher, but the conversation often begins between principal and teacher.

School leaders support teachers' professionalism by sharing feedback with teachers about objectives of lessons, the degree of student engagement, and the behavior of students.

For new principals in particular, it is essential to be active and involved in the classroom as a dependable presence in the student learning process. Through such involvement, the principal can help teachers instill a sense of success for all students—a feeling that is vastly important to improved student performance. (2001, p. 33)

In line with the role of instructional leader, the principal is key to ensuring that teacher observations are as effective as they can be. To do this aspect of the job well, a principal needs an understanding of standards for student learning, an in-depth sense of what good teaching looks like, and strong communication and interpersonal skills (Protheroe, 2002). NAESP recognizes the need to provide training for school leaders in skills such as these. For example, principals need "strong skills in providing open, constructive, and accurate feedback." (2001, p. 25)

Figure 8.1. Traditional and New Paradigms for Teacher Observation

Traditional Paradigm	New Paradigm
Infrequent and brief classroom observations	Frequent observations of varied lessons/practices
Focus on student behavior	Focus on student learning
Focus on classroom management	Focus on effective teaching
Judgments based on personal philosophy and teaching style	Judgments based on evidence of student learning
Focus on lesson plans	Focus on curriculum standards and learning objectives
"One size fits all" observations	Contextually appropriate observations
Single observation method and protocol is used	Multiple methods and protocols are used
Power (supervisory authority) supersedes craft knowledge and expertise	Research-based best practices are the basis of expertise authority
Changes in practice based on principal recommendations	Changes in practice based on professional development goals/plans
Each observation a discrete event	Observations part of a teacher development process linked to goals and prior observation results
Feedback from principal only	Feedback connected to collaborative dialogue with other teachers (Williams et al., 2002, p. 19)

NAESP also encourages principals to engage in reflective practice as another means of refining their skills related to teacher observation. For example, they might ask:

- How often am I in classrooms? What evidence do I see of good teaching and high levels of learning?
- What kinds of feedback do I share with teachers after observing their classes? Does this feedback focus on the teacher's lessons, methods of instruction, and student learning? Does it focus on the extent to which all students were engaged in meaningful/relevant instructional activities? How do I use what I learn from students and student work/performance to help teachers improve their practices? (2001, p. 38)

What Are We Looking For?

To positively impact instruction, there are several aspects of data collection and use that must be carefully structured. Think back to our three key data questions: What are we looking for? How will we look for it? How will we use the data? In planning teacher observations, principals need to carefully define what they are looking for, with three elements especially important:

- Teaching to standards;
- Evidence that students are engaged in learning; and,
- Instructional strategies identified by research as "good teaching."

Teaching to Standards

In today's standards-based educational environment, both principals and teachers need a clear understanding of what students are expected to know and be able to do. Marshall states:

> When a principal visits a classroom, one of the most important things to looks for is whether the teacher is on target with the curriculum. Of course, to answer the question means that the principal must know what exactly the curriculum is.... Teacher supervision can't be efficient and effective until curriculum expectations are clear and widely accepted within the school. (Marshall, 2003, p. 705)

Many districts have worked to develop curricula carefully aligned with their standards. In addition, pacing guides may have been developed. Together these resources provide roadmaps for elements of instruction principals should observe while in classrooms.

These roadmaps are especially helpful when visiting a classroom of a teacher whose students are demonstrating less progress than those of another teacher working at the same grade level or teaching the same content. For example, is the content being taught aligned with guidelines for curriculum content and pacing that have been established? If not, principal-teacher conversation should focus on the reasons why. Your follow-up support might focus on providing opportunities for the teacher to observe in another classroom. Or perhaps the grade-level teachers could meet together to discuss ways to better support low-performing students. Another explanation might be that the teacher pays too little attention to the pacing guide—instead continuing in familiar patterns such as teaching to the textbook. This also requires your attention.

Evidence That Students Are Engaged in Learning

Every principal has gone into classrooms that are vibrant examples of students engaged in learning—and into classrooms in which students' attention is wandering. This is another indicator that should be part of classroom observations. Does the teacher make use of a variety of approaches—whole class as well as small group, encouraging responses from all students, etc.—that generate student participation and enthusiasm? Keep in mind, though, that a "fun" classroom also needs to be standards-based. Students should be engaged in learning the "right stuff," focusing on content that will help them meet standards.

Instructional Strategies Identified as "Good Teaching"

Research is providing an increasingly strong base of information—written in practitioner-relevant language—about good teaching strategies. Protheroe talks about the need for principals to be knowledgeable about this:

> For the teacher observation process to be effective, the principal needs a solid foundation of knowledge about good teaching. The research base on effective teaching suggests components that principals should look for

as they conduct observations. It also serves as a powerful foundation for principal-teacher conversations about good teaching, provides a resource for teachers who are working to strengthen their skills, and guides planning for professional development. (2002, p. 4)

Marshall (2006b) describes his efforts to develop a rubric-based system for teacher observation that focused on key elements of a teacher's responsibilities, provided clear descriptions of teacher behaviors, and could be easily used by teachers and principals as a basis for discussion. Figure 8.2 is the observation sheet he developed for the domain of Monitoring, Assessment, and Follow up. This sheet—along with others covering the domains of Planning and Preparation for Teaching, Classroom Management, Delivery of Instruction, Family and Community Outreach, and Professional Responsibilities—would be used to develop an "end-of-year evaluation based on numerous short, informal, unannounced classroom visits, each followed up with a face-to-face conversation with the teacher" (K. Marshall, personal communication, February 26, 2008). A teacher might exhibit some behaviors classified as expert, while other behaviors might need improvement. This rubric sheet—which Marshall highlights to indicate what he observed—provides a roadmap to areas for teacher improvement.

How Will We Look For It?

Most school districts have a structure for required teacher observations. Many of them are checklist based, and some differentiate between new and experienced teachers. However, many—if not most—of these required approaches have two significant shortcomings. They happen so seldom that they may allow less-than-effective teaching practices to continue through much of the school year, and they are not explicitly tied to principal-teacher conversations that result in individualized teacher development opportunities. Thus, such systems are unlikely to result in a strong follow-up plan for teacher development.

On a positive note, many educators are recognizing the role that effective teacher observation can play in helping teachers continually grow and improve their performance. Stansbury (2001) suggests that teacher observation should be embedded in the day-to-day work of professional growth and classroom practice. Principals should ask themselves, does the approach I am using for teacher observation—or one I am thinking about using—help me to help teachers strengthen their abilities to teach all students to high standards?

Figure 8.2. Monitoring, Assessment, and Follow-Up

The teacher:

4—Expert

- Posts the criteria for proficient work, including rubrics and exemplars, and students internalize them.

- Uses a variety of first-rate assessments to pre-diagnose and continuously monitor students' learning.

- Continuously checks for understanding, unscrambles confusion, and gives specific, helpful feedback.

- Has students set ambitious goals, self-assess and self-monitor, and take responsibility for their progress.

- Frequently posts students' work with rubrics and commentary and uses it to motivate and direct effort.

- Immediately uses interim assessment data to fine-tune teaching, re-teach, and help struggling students.

- Relentlessly follows up with struggling students with time and support to reach proficiency.

- Makes sure that students who need specialized diagnosis and help receive appropriate services ASAP.

- Charts and analyzes assessment data, draws action conclusions, and shares them with others.

- Constantly reflects on the effectiveness of teaching and works every day to improve.

3—Proficient

- Posts clear criteria for proficiency, including rubrics and exemplars of student work.

- Diagnoses students' knowledge and skills up front and uses a variety of assessments during each unit.

- Frequently checks for understanding and gives students helpful feedback if they seem confused.

- Has students set goals, self-assess, and know where they stand academically at all times.

- Regularly posts students' work to make visible and celebrate their progress with respect to standards.

- Uses data from interim assessments to adjust teaching, re-teach, and follow up with failing students.

- Takes responsibility for students who are not succeeding and tenaciously gives them extra help.

- When necessary, refers students for specialized diagnosis and extra help.

- Analyzes data from summative assessments, draws conclusions, and shares them appropriately.
- Reflects on the effectiveness of lessons and units and continuously works to improve them.

2—Needs Improvement

- Tells students some of the qualities that their finished work should exhibit.
- Uses pencil-and-paper quizzes and tests with some open-ended questions to assess student learning.
- Asks questions to see if students understand.
- Urges students to look over their tests, see where they had trouble, and aim to improve those areas.
- Posts some 'A' student work as an example for others.
- Looks over students' tests to see if there is anything that needs to be re-taught.
- Offers students who fail tests some additional time to study and do re-takes.
- Sometimes doesn't refer students promptly for special help, or refers students who don't need it.
- Records students' grades and notices some general patterns for future reference.
- At the end of a teaching unit or semester, thinks about what might have been done better.

1—Does Not Meet Standards

- Expects students to know (or figure out) what it takes to get good grades.
- Uses only multiple-choice and short-answer pencil-and-paper tests to assess student learning.
- Rarely takes time to check for understanding.
- Urges students to work harder and be more careful on future tests.
- Posts only a few samples of 'A' work.
- Looks over unit and final tests to see if there are any lessons for the future.
- Tells students that if they fail a test, that's it; the class has to move on to cover the curriculum.
- Either fails to refer students for special education or refers students who do not need it.
- Records students' grades and moves on with the curriculum.
- When a teaching unit or lesson doesn't go well, chalks it up to experience.

Overall rating: _____ Comments:

Source: Marshall, 2006b

Williams et al. stress that any framework for an observation system should take teachers' individual professional needs into account. The purposes for conducting a specific teacher observation—or series of observations—could include the following:

- *Intervening* to rectify a problem—Expectations for instruction or the appropriate treatment of students are not being met.

- *Coaching* to improve—The teacher is working to refine a specific practice or deal more effectively with a particular situation.

- *Monitoring* the implementation of a program or component of a model—The principal wants to ensure that the program is being implemented as intended (fidelity).

- *Responding* to a teacher's request for assistance in handling a particular situation—The teacher wants suggestions for learning strategies to achieve a specific learning goal or work with a particular type of student.

- *Affirming and reinforcing*—The principal supports the teacher's growth, effectiveness, or success in implementing a new practice.

- *Documenting and recording*—The observer records specific techniques or documents examples of student learning.

These are not discrete purposes; in practice they overlap. The point is that in planning the observation, the principal should have a clear purpose that can be communicated to the teacher and used to prepare, implement, and follow up on the observation. (Williams et al., 2002, pp. 26-27)

Williams et al. also stress that principals should keep in mind other factors—other characteristics—that might vary among teachers in the school:

> Accepting diversity in a staff means recognizing that teachers differ in their ability to examine their own practices and in their openness to having others examine their work. They also differ in the readiness, knowledge, skills, and orientations they bring to the teaching and learning process. Principals must approach the observer role with the same appreciation for teacher diversity that they expect teachers to recognize in their students. This requires a range of observation strategies that are responsive to the differentiated needs of a diverse staff. (2002, pp. 11-12)

Some Approaches to Teacher Observation

Marshall (1996) talks about his personal evolution toward a new approach to teacher observation while he worked as a principal. After becoming increasingly dissatisfied with the information that his district's more formal observations process provided him about teacher knowledge, skills, and performance, he began to add 5-minute visits to classrooms to his everyday schedule, eventually finding that he could manage four or five visits a day. Marshall used these guidelines as he developed his approach to visiting classroom:

- Classroom visits would have to be brief (otherwise they couldn't be frequent and still fit into my hectic schedule) but not *too* brief (because then I'd fail to see what was really going on).

- Visits would have to be frequent; otherwise there woudn't be enough of them to balance specific praise with specific criticism.
- Visits would have to be random and unannounced, or I would risk seeing only specially prepared, glamorized lessons.
- I would need to give feedback soon after every visit, or teachers would be left guessing about conclusions I had drawn.
- The feedback should be presented face to face to make it as nonthreatening as possible and to allow for conversation about what was happening in the classroom. (Marshall, 1996, p. 339)

Marshall provided feedback to each of the teachers visited—ideally, by the end of the same day. In his view, these visits helped to enrich his relationships with teachers and to build his knowledge of both curriculum and instruction in his school.

Neide (1996) talks about periodically focusing on a very narrow range of teacher behaviors when making short classroom visits. For example, she suggests that observing and documenting how a teacher provides positive and negative feedback could be the purpose of an observation.

Peery talks about her use of a transcription process for longer observations as a supplement to the district-supplied checklist-type teacher observation form. She uses these transcripts to jumpstart conversations with teachers:

I let the teacher's comments guide the conversation unless there is something I was alarmed about, such as student safety, blatant disregard for school procedures, or curriculum and instruction practices I could not support.

Teachers notice things in my transcripts that I would never see: improvements they want to make in a lesson, for example....The transcripts and conversations then provide the impetus for inquiry. (2002, p. 26)

How Will We Use the Data?

Follow-up from a classroom observation deserves careful attention. In Van der Linde's view, "The follow-up discussion sometimes provides the most important situation for the collection of further data, because teachers are now in a situation where they are able to explain their behavior" (1998, p. 332).

> "The key to success as a clinical supervisor is to first understand the teacher's perception of the data and its meaning" (Pajak, 2001, p. 241).

Peery's Transcription Process

- Be a careful observer. Write down all you see and hear for a period of at least 30 minutes or one complete class activity. Be sure to note facial expressions, body language, and actual words spoken by the teacher and the students. Note the time in the margins periodically.

- Provide the transcript to the teacher within 24 hours. Type it after the observation if it's not legible . . . or provide a photocopy.

- Invite or require the teacher to confer with you as follow-up.... Allow the teacher to choose the time of the conference unless you have fairly serious concerns. If you have serious concerns, schedule the conference as soon as possible which could be at the end of the class period or during the teacher's lunch the same day, if necessary.

- In the conference, ask the teacher, "What did you see in the transcript? What is worthy of discussion?" If possible, let the teacher lead the discussion. This is where the real learning takes place. Plan for ongoing follow-up.

- For a teacher you have some concerns about, arrange a longer follow-up visit. Allow the teacher to pick the date and time and look for improvements in things that you and the teacher have already discussed.

- Confer after this observation and conduct an unannounced one shortly afterwards as well. Continue the cycle of observations and conferences until the problems you noted are under control or you decide to take some other action. (Peery, 2002, p. 27)

Marshall talks about conversations he had with teachers as follow-ups to short and frequent visits he made to classrooms:

> I found that verbal feedback worked best. When I occasionally gave feedback in a written note or an email, the teacher rarely responded, so there was no dialogue. I also found that I was much more guarded about putting negative feedback in writing because it was more permanent (and more threatening) and because I couldn't judge the teacher's mood and ability to absorb a critical comment. Written feedback also deprived me of the rich and substantive conversations that often grew out of face-to-face feedback talks. So I stuck almost entirely to verbal follow-ups, usually stand-up conversations in such informal settings as the teacher's classroom during a free period, in a corridor, by the copy machine, or while walking to our cars after school. These talks lasted an average of 3 to 5 minutes.... The feedback conversations played an important ethical role in this system: they gave teachers a chance to clue me in on the broader context of a particular teaching moment, to correct me if I misheard or got the wrong idea, and to push back if they disagreed with a criticism. (2003, p. 704)

He also is clear that principals need to provide objective, truthful feedback to teachers they observe:

> Some principals sugarcoat criticism and give inflated scores for fear of hurting feelings. This does not help teachers improve. The kindest thing a principal can do

for an underperforming teacher is to give candid, evidence-based feedback and robust follow-up support. (2008, p. 1)

Glanz considers feedback an integral part of the observation process, and he adds an interesting thought for principals to keep in mind:

Observation is a two-step process: first, to describe what has occurred, and second, to interpret what it means. Too often, we jump into what has been termed the *interpretation trap*. We jump to conclusions about a particular behavior before describing that behavior. When we interpret first, we not only lose description of the event, but also create communication difficulties that might result in teacher resistance. (2004, p. 48)

Obviously, translating your observations into opportunities for teacher development is also important. Williams et al. talk about the link between observation and professional development: "We have traditionally viewed teacher observation as but one strategy for supporting teacher development; we now must think of it as the foundation for teacher development" (2002, p. 14).

Holland reminds principals to explicitly make the link between teacher formative evaluation—in particular, observations that together contribute to the data base needed for evaluation—and teacher development. These observations should be used to "identify a teacher's current levels of knowledge and skill and use them as the basis for a coherent and documented plan for that teacher's continued learning and professional development" (2005, p. 72).

Supports provided for teachers might include resource materials, peers who can serve as coaches or who themselves can be observed, formal professional development programs, or independent projects such as action research.

> The observation process should be embedded in the overall professional development process, with clear connections to long-term development goals. The instructional leader's approach is based on this central question: "What is the best approach for helping this teacher learn and enhance his or her practice given the learning goals for students, given this teacher in this situation?" (Williams et al., 2002, p. 45)

Introducing a New Approach to Classroom Observation

For teachers accustomed to annual, checklist-driven approaches to classroom observation, a move to more frequent, often-unannounced principal visits may be seen as a major shift in practice. Williams et al. discuss the need for principals to address such considerations:

Changing any process within the school requires careful planning based on many factors. Modifying the teacher observation process is no exception; indeed, because it focuses on one of the most private aspects of schooling—what goes on behind the closed doors of classrooms—these factors can be quite complex. In some schools, these changes involve relatively minor shifts in a teacher observation and instructional improvement process that is well accepted. In other settings, however, introducing a teacher observation process aimed at improving instructional practice and student learning represents a major organizational change that involves substantial changes in the culture of the school. (Williams et al., 2002, p. 39)

Implications for Our School: Questions for Discussion and Reflection

- How would we "grade" the linkage between teacher observation and teacher development in our school?

- Are there elements of teacher observation as it is currently practiced here that support teacher growth and development?

- Are there elements that need attention? What are some ways we could improve these?

Follow-up and Action Items

_____

_____

_____

_____

_____

_____

_____

_____

_____

_____

_____

_____

_____

_____

_____

_____

_____

Chapter 9

Summing Up

> "Effective leaders are skilled at focusing on the most important data and bringing it to the forefront so it can be analyzed to inform changes that make sense for the school's staff and community." (National Association for Elementary School Principals, 2008, p. 99)

Just a few examples of ways in which data use can support school improvement efforts have been presented in this resource. You and your staff could probably brainstorm dozens more in just a few minutes. Remember that such endeavors need not be "big" projects. Many times the data question can focus on a small and manageable concern. However, addressing this small concern through careful study can often have big payoffs. Here are some additional examples of ways your school might use data.

Ask new teachers how things are going—but in an organized way. Focus on things they feel are particularly helpful in providing them with support, as well as on things they see as barriers. Then use this data to identify ways you and the rest of the staff can provide stronger support for new teachers.

New teachers can be encouraged to assess their own use of instructional strategies by paying special attention to a few students. They should ask themselves: Are these students engaged or not? Have they all demonstrated understanding of instructions and assignments? Are there lessons that seem to go especially well for them—or not so well? Spending time with a new teacher to talk about how to structure these observations and then to discuss what they felt these observations told them can help to improve instruction while building data analysis skills.

Helping students learn how to use data to support their own learning is another application of data use and analysis. For example, Gregory and Kuzmich (2004) suggest that students be encouraged to self-assess their work using teacher-provided rubrics—then use the data they collect to improve.

One elementary school uses a graphic display of data to help generate questions intended to help keep children's progress on track. Hundreds of color-coded cards grouped by grade level line the "Assessment Wall" in the office of the school's literacy coordinator. Each card represents a student (names on the back for privacy purposes) and his/her progress through assessment Strategic Teaching and Evaluation of Progress (STEPS). Teachers meet twice a month with the coordinator to review status and progress, "group and regroup pupils according to the progress they are making, identify pupils who are reading below grade level, and—most importantly—exchange intervention strategies to help those who are struggling" (Pardini, 2000).

One final example—A principal concerned about the amount of whole-class, teacher-directed instruction he was seeing during his classroom visits decided to include teachers in the observation process. Time that had been set aside for professional development was reallocated to having teachers do "multiple pop-in visits to as many classrooms as they could reasonably visit in one class period" (McEnery, 2005, p. 45). Teachers were asked to use an observation form provided by the principal to record what they observed teachers and students doing. After pulling together and sharing data from these multiple observations, the principal provided time for teachers to discuss their observations. In his view, the observations and the resulting discussions provided "motivation for change" (p. 46), with teachers asking for professional development focused on use of fewer teacher-directed strategies.

Effective data use doesn't simply support efforts to make good decisions; it also helps to build staff capacity. Goldring and Berends (2009) describe it as building community through organizational learning. Earl and Katz (2006) agree and view effective data use as an important element of professional learning communities. In such schools, educators collaborate to problem solve, a setting the authors characterize as a "culture of inquiry," and an important role for principals is helping teachers and other staff members develop an "inquiry habit of mind." They need to feel comfortable with having sometimes difficult discussions focused on problems identified through data use and also to consider themselves capable of identifying solutions to these.

"Clearly, data analysis is not a panacea that will solve every problem in a school. But when properly focused and implemented, data analysis is one tool that a school's staff can use to help raise educational achievement." (Wade, 2001, p. 2)

Earlier in this book, it was stressed that some conditions must be in place if a school is to move forward with systematic data use for improvement. Some of these—such as time for teachers to work together—can be made available on an ad hoc basis around a specific project. Others, in particular an environment of trust, are foundational to a school staff's ability to work together effectively as a community in support of student learning. Ensuring these conditions are met will fall primarily on the principal's shoulders.

In addition, principals should take the lead in demonstrating the value of data use to school improvement. Boudett and Steele talk about the importance of this:

> Challenging as it is, using data to improve teaching and learning is possible. In our experience, the key lies in building a school culture in which faculty members collaborate regularly and make instructional decisions based on evidence about students' skills and understanding. (2007, p. 2)

They also talk about the first step—Prepare—of the Data Wise process, a cyclical approach to data use for school improvement. In this phase,

> School leaders typically face two critical challenges: communicating the need for a data initiative and creating data teams that are equipped to lead the work. The leaders we studied confront these challenges in two ways: by making data relevant, and by giving their data teams time to develop the skills and systems they need to be successful. (Boudett & Steele, 2007, p. 1)

Finally, while data use can provide a critical support for school improvement efforts, it must be accompanied with hard, focused work since "the leap from data to action is not simple" (Knapp et al., 2006, p. 18). As the school leader, perhaps the most difficult—and most necessary—part of your job is ensuring that this work happens.

Implications for Our School:
Questions for Discussion and Reflection

- Discuss challenges in your school that might benefit from a more focused use of data.
- Select one or two and create an action plan that will enable your school to move forward with addressing the challenges through data use.

Follow-up and Action Items

_____

_____

_____

_____

_____

_____

_____

_____

_____

_____

_____

_____

_____

_____

_____

_____

_____

_____

_____

References

Administration for Children and Families. (2003). *The program manager's guide to evaluation.* Retrieved from http://www.acf.hhs.gov/programs/opre/other_resrch/pm_guide_eval/reports/pmguide/pmguide_toc.html

Aldersebaes, I., Potter, J., & Hamilton, N. (2000). *Programs don't—people do: Insights into schoolwide change.* Portland, OR: Northwest Regional Educational Laboratory.

Allensworth, E. M., & Easton, J. Q. (2007). *What matters for staying on track and graduating in Chicago public high schools.* Chicago: Consortium on Chicago School Research at the University of Chicago. Retrieved from http://ccsr.uchicago.edu/content/publications.php?pub_id=116

Apthorp, H. (2007, Spring). RTI model uses data to improve instruction "here & now." *Changing Schools,* 8-9.

Arlington Public Schools. (1999). *A framework for systematic accountability and evaluation.* Arlington, VA: Author.

Arnberger, K., & Shoop, R. J. (2008, January). Responding to need. *Principal Leadership,* 51-54.

Aschbacher, P. R., Koency, G., & Schacter, J. (1995). *Los Angeles Learning Center alternative assessment guidebook.* Los Angeles: National Center for Research on Evaluation, Standards, and Student Testing.

Balfanz, R., Herzog, L., Mac Iver, & D. J. (2006) *Preventing student disengagement and keeping students on the graduation track in high poverty middle-grades: Early identification and effective interventions.* Retrieved from http://www.mgforum.org/News/MembersSpeak/Article-MacIver.pdf

Bergeson, T., Heuschel, M. A., Harmon, B., Gill, D. H., Alig, P., & Middling, T. (2006). *Using Response to Intervention (RTI) for Washington's students.* Olympia, WA: Washington Office of Superintendent of Public Instruction.

Black, P., & Wiliam, D. (1998, October). Inside the black box: Raising standards through classroom assessment. *Phi Delta Kappan.* Retrieved from www.pdkintl.org/kappan/kbla9810.htm

Boudett, K., & Moody, L. (2005). Organizing for collaborative work. In K. P. Boudett, E. A. City, & R. J. Murnane (Eds.), *Data Wise: A step-by-step guide to using assessment results to improve teaching and learning.* Cambridge, MA: Harvard Education Press.

Boudett, K. P., & Steele, J. L. (Eds.). (2007). *Data Wise in action: Stories of schools using data to improve teaching and learning.* Cambridge, MA: Harvard University Press.

Brown-Chidsey, R. (2007, October). No more 'waiting to fail': How Response to Intervention works and why it is needed. *Educational Leadership,* 40-46.

Canter, A., Klotz, M. B., & Cowan, K. (2008, February). Response to Intervention: The future for secondary schools. *Principal Leadership,* 12-15.

Cawelti, G., & Protheroe, N. (2001). *High student achievement: How six school districts changed into high-performance systems.* Arlington, VA: Educational Research Service.

Center for Comprehensive School Reform and Improvement. (2006). *Program evaluation for the practitioner: Using evaluation as a school improvement strategy.* Washington, DC: Author.

Cervone, L., & Martinez-Miller, P. (2007). Classroom walkthroughs as a catalyst for school improvement. *Leadership Compass, 4*(4). Retrieved from http://www.naesp.org/resources/2/Leadership_Compass/2007/LC2007v4n4a2.pdf

Champion, R. (2002, Summer). Choose the right data for the job: A good evaluation measures the same thing from different angles. *Journal of Staff Development,* 78-79.

Champion, R. (2004, Summer). Taking measure: Frequently asked questions from the evaluator's mailbox. *Journal of Staff Development.* Retrieved from www.nsdc.org/library/publications/jsd/champion253.cfm

Cicchinelli, L., & Barley, Z. (1999). *Evaluating for success: Comprehensive school reform: An evaluation guide for districts and schools.* Aurora, CO: Mid-continent Research for Education and Learning.

City, E. A., Kagle, M., & Teoh, M. B. (2005). Examining instruction. In K. P. Boudette, E. A. City, & R. J. Murnane (Eds.), *Data Wise: A step-by-step guide to using assessment results to improve teaching and learning.* Cambridge, MA: Harvard Education Press.

Creighton, T. B. (2007). *Schools and data: The educator's guide for using data to improve decision making* (2nd ed.). Thousand Oaks, CA: Corwin Press.

Cromey, A., & and Hanson, M. (2000). *An exploratory analysis of school-based student assessment systems.* Naperville, IL: North Central Regional Education Laboratory. Retrieved from http://www.ncrel.org/re/eval/mi/analysis.htm

Damian, C. (2000). Facing—and embracing—the assessment challenge. *ENC Focus 7*(2), 16-17.

Datnow, A., Park, V., & Wohlstetter, P. (2007). *Achieving with data.* Los Angeles: Center on Educational Governance, Rossier School of Education, University of Southern California.

Depka, E. (2006). *The data guidebook for teachers and leaders: Tools for continuous improvement.* Thousand Oaks, CA: Corwin Press.

Downey, C. J., Steffy, B. E., Poston, W. K., Jr., & English, F. W. (2009). *50 ways to close the achievement gap* (3rd ed.). Thousand Oaks, CA: Corwin Press.

Earl, L., & Katz, S. (2006). *Leading schools in a data-rich world: Harnessing data for school improvement.* Thousand Oaks, CA: Corwin Press.

Earl, L. M., & Katz, S. (2008). *Leading schools in a data-rich world* (Facilitator's guide). Thousand Oaks, CA: Corwin Press.

Earl, L. M., & Katz, S. (2010). Creating a culture of inquiry. In A. M. Blankstein, P. D. Houston, & R. W. Cole (Eds.), *Data Enhanced Leadership.* Thousand Oaks, CA: Corwin Press, Hope Foundation, and American Association of School Administrators.

Edwards, S. W., & Edwards, R. (2007). *The principal's role in dropout prevention: Seven key principles.* Clemson, SC: National Dropout Prevention Center.

Georgia Department of Education. (2006). Identifying at-risk students in your school. Atlanta, GA: Author.

Glanz, J. (2004). *The assistant principal's handbook: Strategies for success.* Thousand Oaks, CA: Corwin Press.

Goldring, E., & Berends, M. (2009). *Leading with data: Pathways to improve your school.* Thousand Oaks, CA: Corwin Press.

Gregory, G. H., & Kuzmich, L. (2004). *Data driven differentiation in the standards-based classroom.* Thousand Oaks, CA: Corwin Press.

Guskey, T. R. (2002, March). Does it make a difference? Evaluating professional development. *Educational Leadership*, 45-51.

Hall, S. (2008). *A principal's guide to implementing Response to Intervention.* Thousand Oaks, CA: Corwin Press.

Hammond, O. (2006, Spring). The evaluation corner. *Pacific Educator*, 11.

Hammond, C., Smink, J., & Drew, S. (2007). *Dropout risk factors and exemplary programs: A technical report.* Clemson, SC: National Dropout Prevention Center at Clemson University and Communities in Schools, Inc. Retrieved from http://www.dropoutprevention.org/resource/major_reports/communities_in_schools.htm

Heppen, J. B., & Therriault, S. B. (2008). *Developing early warning systems to identify potential high school dropouts.* Washington, DC: National High School Center. Retrieved from http://www.betterhighschools.com/pubs/ews_guide.pdf

Heritage, M. & Yeagely, R. (2005). Data use and school improvement: Challenges and prospects. In J. L. Herman & E. H. Haertel (Eds.), *Uses and misuses of data for educational accountability and improvement.* Malden, MA: Blackwell Publishing.

Herman, J. L., & Winters, L. (1992). *Tracking your school's success: A guide to sensible evaluation.* Newbury Park, CA: Corwin Press.

Holcomb, E. (2004). *Getting excited about data* (2nd ed.). Thousand Oaks, CA: Corwin Press.

Holland, P. (2005, January). The case for expanding standards for teacher evaluation to include an instructional supervision perspective. *Journal of Personnel Evaluation in Education*, 67-77.

Horowitz, S. H. (2005, July). Response to Intervention: A primer. *LD News.* Retrieved from http://www.ncld.org/index.php?option=content&task= view&id=598

Howard, L. (2004). *Essentials for principals: Effective program evaluation.* Alexandria, VA: National Association of Elementary School Principals and Educational Research Service.

Jandris, T. P. (2001). *Essentials for principals: Data-based decision making.* Alexandria, VA: National Association of Elementary School Principals and Educational Research Service.

Jerald, C. D. (2006). *Identifying potential dropouts: Key lessons for building an early warning data system.* Washington, DC: Achieve, Inc., American Diploma Project Network. Retrieved from http://www.achieve.org/files/ FINAL-dropouts_0.pdf

Johnson, E., Mellard, D. F., Fuchs, D., & McKnight, M. A. (2006). *Responsiveness to Intervention (RTI): How to do it.* Lawrence, KS: National Research Center on Learning Disabilities. Retrieved from http://nrcld.org/rti_manual/

Johnson, J. H. (2000, Spring). Data-driven school improvement. *Journal of School Improvement.* Retrieved from http://www.ncacasi.org/jsi/ 2000v1i1/data_driven

Johnson, R. S. (2002). *Using data to close the achievement gap: How to measure equity in our schools.* Thousand Oaks, CA: Corwin Press.

Johnston, J., Knight, M., & Miller, L. (2007, Spring). Finding time for teams. *Journal of Staff Development,* 14-18.

Kaufman, R., Guerra, I., & Platt, W. A. (2006). *Practical evaluation for educators: Finding what works and what doesn't.* Thousand Oaks, CA: Corwin Press.

Killion, J. (2002). *Assessing impact: Evaluating staff development.* Oxford, OH: National Staff Development Council.

Killion, J., & Bellamy, G. T. (2000, Winter). On the job: Data analysts focus school improvement efforts. *Journal of Staff Development.* Retrieved from http://www.nsdc.org/educatorindex.htm

Knapp, M. A., Swinnerton, J. A., Copland, M. A., & Monpas-Huber, J. (2006). *Data-informed leadership in education: A research report in collaboration with the Wallace Foundation.* Seattle, WA: Center for the Study of Teaching and Policy, University of Washington. Retrieved from http://depts.washington.edu/ctpmail/PDFs/DataInformed-Nov1.pdf

Langer, G. M., Colton, A. B., & Goff, L. (2003). *Collaborative analysis of student work: Improving teaching and learning.* Alexandria, VA: Association of Supervision and Curriculum Development.

Linan-Thompson, S., Vaughn, S., Prater, K., and Cirino, P. T. (2006, September/October). The response to intervention of English language learners at risk for reading problems. *Journal of Reading Disabilities,* 390-398.

Love, N. (Ed.). (2009). *Using data to improve learning for all: A collaborative inquiry approach.* Thousand Oaks, CA: Corwin Press.

Marshall, K. (1996, January). How I confronted HSPS (Hyperactive Superficial Principal Syndrome) and began to deal with the heart of the matter. *Phi Delta Kappan,* 336-345.

Marshall, K. (2003, May). Recovering from HSPS (Hyperactive Superficial Principal Syndrome): A progress report. *Phi Delta Kappan,* 701-709.

Marshall, K. (2006a). Interim assessments: Keys to successful implementation. New York: New Leaders for New Schools. Retrieved from http://www.marshallmemo.com/articles/Interim%20Assmt%20Report%20Apr.%2012,%2006.pdf

Marshall, K. (2006b, September/October). Teacher evaluation rubrics: The why and the how. *EDge Magazine.* Retrieved from http://www.marshallmemo.com/articles/EDge%20Rubrics%20Jan.%2025,%2006.doc

Marshall, K. (2008, September). Interim assessments: A user's guide. *Phi Delta Kappan,* 64-68.

Martinez, R. S., & Nellis, L. M. (2008). Response to Intervention: A schoolwide approach for promoting academic wellness for all students. In B. Doll & J. A. Cummings (Eds.), *Transforming School Mental Health Services* (pp. 143-164). Thousand Oaks, CA: Corwin Press.

Martinez, R. S., Nellis, L. M., & Prendergast, K. A. (2006, Fall). Closing the achievement gap series: Part II Response to Intervention (RTI)—Basic elements, practical applications, and policy recommendations. *Education Policy Brief.* Retrieved from http://ceep.indiana.edu/projects/PDF/PB_V4N8_Fall_2006_AchievementGap.pdf

McAfee, O., Leong, D., & Bodrova, E. (2004). *Basics of assessment: A primer for early childhood educators.* Washington, DC: National Association for the Education of Young Children.

McEnery, D. (2005, May). Getting out of the way: A lesson in change. *Principal Leadership,* 42-46.

McNamara, C. (1998). *Basic guide to program evaluation.* Retrieved from http://www.managementhelp.org/evaluatn/fnl_eval.htm

McNeely, M. (2006), *Real-time evaluation strategies.* Presentation at Building State Capacity to Improve Schools: CSR & Title I conference hosted by the U.S. Department of Education. Atlanta, GA (May 11-12, 2006).

Mellard, D. F., & Johnson, E. (2008). *RTI: A practitioner's guide to implementing Response to Intervention.* Thousand Oaks, CA: Corwin Press and Alexandria, VA: National Association of Elementary School Principals.

Mid-continent Research for Education and Learning. (2000). *Evaluation.* Aurora, CO: Author.

Mishook, J., Foley, E., Thompson, J., & Kubiak, M. (2008, Winter). Beyond test scores: Leading indicators for education. *Voices in Urban Education.* Retrieved from http://www.annenberginstitute.org/VUE/winter08/Mishook.php

Meyers, E., & Rust, F. O. (2000). The test doesn't tell all: How teachers know that their students are learning. *Education Week* (June 30, 2000), 34, 37.

National Association of Elementary School Principals. (2001). *Leading learning communities: Standards for what principals should know and be able to do.* Alexandria, VA: Author.

National Association of Elementary School Principals. (2008). *Leading learning communities: Standards for what principals should know and be able to do (2nd Ed.).* Alexandria, VA: Author.

National Association of State Directors of Special Education and Council of Administrators of Special Education. (2006). *Response to Intervention: NASDSE and CASE white paper on RtI.* Retrieved from http://waccbd. org/RtiResources/RtIAnAdministratorsPerspective1-06.pdf

National Center for Learning Disabilities. (n.d.). *What is Response to Intervention?* Retrieved from http://www.ncld.org/content/ view/1221/398/

National Research Center on Learning Disabilities. (n.d.). Core findings about Response to Intervention. *LD InfoZone.* Retrieved from http://www. ncld.org/content/view/1220/389/

Neide, J. (1996, September). Supervision of student teachers: Objective observation. *Journal of Physical Education, Recreation & Dance,* 14-18.

Niyogi, N. S. (1995). *The intersection of instruction and assessment: The classroom.* Princeton, NJ: Educational Testing Service.

North Carolina Department of Public Instruction. (1999). *Classroom assessment: Linking instruction and assessment.* Raleigh, NC: Author.

North Dakota Department of Public Instruction. (n.d.). *Data based decision making.* Retrieved from http://www.dpi.state.nd.us/speced/personnel/ decision.shtm

O'Cummings, M., Heppen, J. B., Therriault, S. B., Johnson, A., & Fryer, L. (2010). *Early Warning System Tool 2.0.* Washington, DC: National High School Center. Retrieved from http://www.betterhighschools. org/EWSTool.aspx

Pajak, E. (2001, May/June). Clinical supervision in a standards-based environment: Opportunities and challenges. *Journal of Teacher Education,* 233-243.

Pam_I_Am. (2007, February 27). JEB Stuart High School [Web log comment]. Retrieved from http://askville.amazon.com/JEB-Stuart-High-School/AnswerDetails.do?requestId=1288337&responseId=128 9495

Pardini, P. (2000, Winter). Six examples of data-driven decision making at work. *Journal of Staff Development.* Retrieved from http://www.nsdc. org/library/publications/jsd/pardini211.cfm

Peery, A. (2002, November). Beyond inservice. *Principal Leadership*, 22-28.

Peltzman, A., & Jerald, C. (2006, December). High standards and high graduation rates. *The State Education Standard*, 7-13.

Philadelphia Education Fund. (n.d.a.). *Keeping middle grades students on track to graduation.* Retrieved from http://www.philaedfund.org/on_track/index.htm

Philadelphia Education Fund. (n.d.b.). *Guidelines for looking at student work.* Retrieved from www.philaedfund.org/slcweb/guideli.htm

Protheroe, N. (2002). *The role of teacher observation in promoting instructional improvement.* Arlington, VA: Educational Research Service.

Reeves, D. (2004, April). Questions and answers from the real world. *Center for Performance Assessment Monthly Email Newsletter.* Retrieved from http://www.makingstandardswork.com/ResourceCtr/enewsletters/enewsletter0404.htm#data

Roderick, M. (1993). *The path to dropping out: Evidence for intervention.* Westport, CT: Auburn House.

Roderick, M. (1994, Winter). Grade retention and the school dropout: Investigating the association. *American Educational Research Journal,* 729-759.

Rumberger, R. W., & Sun, A. L. (2008). *Why students drop out of school: A review of 25 Years of research.* Santa Barbara, CA: California Dropout Research Project. Retrieved from http://lmri.ucsb.edu/dropouts/download.php?file=researchreport15.pdf

Sanders, J. R., & Sullins, C. D. (2006). *Evaluating school programs: An evaluator's guide.* Thousand Oaks, CA: Corwin Press.

Sindelar, N. W. (2011). *Assessment powered teaching.* Thousand Oaks, CA: Corwin Press.

Sparks, D. (2000, Winter). Data should be used to select the most results-oriented initiatives: An interview with Mike Schmoker. *Journal of Staff Development.* Retrieved from http://www.nsdc.org/educatorindex.htm

Sparks, E., Johnson, J. L., & Akos, P. (2008). *Ninth grade dropout risk factors and information for identifying effective practices.* Paper presented at the meeting of the American Educational Research Association, New York, NY.

Standerfer, L. (2005, December). Staff development: Finding the right fit. *Principal Leadership*, 18.

Stansbury, K. (2001, Spring). The role of formative assessment in induction programs. *Reflections*, 1-2.

Sugai, G. (2007). *RTI: Reasons, practices, systems, and considerations* (presentation of the OSEP Center on Positive Behavioral Interventions and Supports).

Thornton, B., & Perreault, G. (2002, March). Becoming a data-based leader: An introduction. *NASSP Bulletin*.

Van der Linde, C. H. (1998, Winter). Clinical supervision in teacher evaluation: A pivotal factor in the quality management of education. *Education*, 328-334.

Vaughn Gross Center for Reading and Language Arts Austin. (2007, October). Progress monitoring: An essential step in the assessment cycle. *Texas Reading First Quarterly*, 2, 4.

W.K. Kellogg Foundation. (1998). *W.K. Kellogg Foundation evaluation handbook*. Battle Creek, MI: Author.

Wade, H. W. (2001). Data inquiry and analysis for educational reform (*ERIC Digest 153*). Retrieved from https://scholarsbank.uoregon.edu/dspace/bitstream/1794/3376/1/digest153.pdf

Walser, N. (2007, January/February). Response to Intervention. *Harvard Education Letter*. Retrieved from http://www.hepg.ore/hel/article/239

Weiss, J. (2007). *Conditions for student success: The cycle of continuous instructional improvement*. NewSchools Venture Fund.

Williams, M., Cray, M., Millen, E., & Protheroe, N. (2002). *Essentials for principals: Effective teacher observations*. Alexandria, VA: National Association of Elementary School Principals.

Yap, K., Aldersebaes, I., Railsback, J., Shaughnessy, J., & Speth, T. (2000). *Evaluating whole-school reform efforts: A guide for district and school staff*. Portland, OR: Northwest Regional Educational Laboratory.